Auditing Social Media

Auditing Social Media

A Governance and Risk Guide

PETER R. SCOTT, APR

J. MIKE JACKA, CIA, CPCU, CLU, CPA

WILEY

John Wiley & Sons, Inc.

Published by John Wiley & Sons, Inc., Hoboken, New Jersey.

Published simultaneously in Canada.

For general information on our other products and services or for technical support, please contact our Customer Care Department within the United States at (800) 762-2974, outside the United States at (317) 572-3993 or fax (317) 572-4002.

Wiley also publishes its books in a variety of electronic formats. Some content that appears in print may not be available in electronic books. For more information about Wiley products, visit our Web site at www.wiley.com.

Library of Congress Cataloging-in-Publication Data:

Scott, Peter R.,
    Auditing social media : a governance and risk guide/Peter R. Scott, J. Mike Jacka.
      p.   cm.
    Includes index.
    ISBN 978-1-118-06175-6 (cloth); ISBN 978-1-118-06369-9 (ebk);
    ISBN 978-1-118-06370-5 (ebk); ISBN 978-1-118-06371-2 (ebk)
      1. Internet marketing.   2. Social media.   3. Business enterprises—Computer networks.   4. Customer relations—Technological innovations.
I. Jacka, J. Mike.   II. Title.
    HF5415.1265.S394 2011
    658.8'72—dc22   2010053514

Printed in the United States of America.

10 9 8 7 6 5 4 3 2 1

To my father for his perseverance and generosity,
to my mother for her strength and courage,
and to Taberi, my wife, for everything
—*Peter*

To Sally and Dan, who opened my eyes to
what was going on
—*Mike*

Contents

Foreword

As I look back on my career at Microsoft, I feel fortunate to have had a front-row seat to witness an incredible shift in how people and organizations communicate and interact. I started at Microsoft in October 1994—about a year after America Online released AOL 1.0 for Windows. As early adopters of social media, Microsoft's "technical evangelist," Robert Scoble, emerged as a social media pioneer, blogging and producing videos of our employees and products as part of Microsoft's Channel 9 MSDN Video team. Since then, we've led the way in embracing the power of online communities.

Today, people around the world are sharing their opinions and experiences about practically everything and anything. What started out as small groups of like-minded people talking about their profession and passions has transformed into an unbridled content democracy. Anyone with Internet access can readily voice his or her opinion, create multiple forms of content, create new products, and—in their own way—change the world.

Over the past few years, organizations around the world have been trying to figure out how to enter the social media pool. Some decided to jump in and quickly learn how to swim. Others were pushed into the deep end and figured it out after thrashing around a bit. And there are even those who chose to stay out of the water, hoping to avoid risk. Unfortunately, if you believe you can simply avoid social media—you can't. You or your organization can choose not to participate, but that doesn't mean people are not talking about you, your products, your programs, your customer service, or the people within your organization. So while there are risks in engaging your stakeholders using social media, there are also serious risks in avoiding it altogether.

What makes the book you're reading unique from most books written for internal auditors is that this book is a collaboration between an internal auditor and a social media practitioner. It provides two different perspectives, but one common message. The end result is a guide to help internal auditors and other leaders throughout the organization collaborate to identify the opportunities and risks of social media as a communication medium. Mike and Pete also provide the details of how to create an effective strategy, governance structure, metrics, and audit program to help provide the assurance, insight, and objectivity necessary for success.

As the use of social media continues to transform within organizations, it's not a matter of *if* but *when* internal auditors will need to play a role. This book is a "must read" for anyone who wants to have a seat at the table and help develop a program that is based on sound business principles.

Rod Winters,
General Manager Finance Operations, Microsoft USA
2009–2010 Global Chairman of The Institute of
Internal Auditors

Acknowledgments

P eter would like to thank Ted Murphy, CEO and founder of IZEA, Inc. Ted's vision, creativity, and perseverance serves as an inspiration to achieve great things. Ted's constant innovation and "disruption with a smile" has forever changed the future of social media. He would also like to thank his friends, colleagues, and fellow board members of the Orlando Chapter of the Public Relations Society of America. It is truly an honor to serve and learn from such exceptional professionals.

Mike would like to thank Paulette Keller and Stan Sherman, who constantly inundated him with concepts, articles, blogs, updates, and various other information on the rapidly evolving world of social media.

And both authors would like to thank the staff and leadership of The Institute of Internal Auditors and The Institute of Internal Auditors Research Foundation, not only for their support throughout this project, but also for the opportunity to work with them in various projects throughout the years. They would also like to thank the team at Wiley for all their expertise and guidance.

Introduction

*Why Should Anyone Care
about Social Media?*

As you are reading this, it is very probable that someone somewhere is writing about your organization.

Why should you care? People have written about organizations, their products and services, and how they conduct business seemingly forever and, except in rare occasions, it hasn't really been a significant risk. Hundreds of years ago a nameless "accountant" was writing about his "organization" by recording entries in Sumerian that would probably be read only by an appointee of the king. A couple of hundred years ago some Colonial American may have been writing a tract about the poor handling he received at the hands of the local cobbler. As recently as a few years ago, your worst-case scenario may have been a disgruntled employee trying to convince a publisher to print his tell-all book about your organization.

So, if someone is writing about your organization today, why should you be any more concerned than you were in those years long ago?

Because every word that is being typed about your organization by every person who has a nasty or kind thing to say has the potential to be read in the homes, haunts, huts, and hideouts of billions of people throughout the world.

In the movie *The Music Man*, the Ladies Guild (in the inspired tune "Pick-a-Little, Talk-a-Little," where images of the busybodies are interspersed with a group of chickens) gossips about the goings on of Marian the librarian. Your organization is Marian, and social media is the Ladies Guild. However, rather than disinformation being spread at the speed of sound throughout a small town in Iowa, the information about your organization is being spread at the speed of light throughout the world.

And it is amazingly pervasive. A little old lady from Pasadena is telling all her Facebook friends (a group that is scattered globally) that your soap gave her shingles. A struggling rock band has prominently placed your organization's name in its new song "Death to the Corporation," and the associated YouTube video is about to go viral. A preadolescent, a "tween," has tweeted on Twitter that she will shop at your store forever because Justin Heartthrob just tweeted that he liked a shirt he bought there. A blogger who thinks nostalgia is yesterday's dinner has mentioned he never heard of your 75-year-old organization until last week and laments how the upstarts in the industry are degrading its quality. A group of eco-terrorists are flaming your discussion page because they mistakenly believe your organization is supporting the destruction of dolphins in Japanese fishing towns.

That is why you and your organization need to be aware of the previously solitary scribblings of your customers. Whether these comments are intentional or inadvertent, they can have a substantive impact on the bottom line—whether that is in profit and loss, brand equity, or share price. Because an organization cannot control the conversation the way it did in the past, there is a clear need to have a comprehensive understanding of the medium, evaluate the opportunities and risks of social media, and develop a strategic approach that best addresses these issues.

So how do you respond to this burgeoning array of communication? We see three different types of response by organizations.

The first are like ostriches. These organizations ignore social media, considering it not worthy of their time, sticking their heads in the sand and refusing to move forward. These are the organizations that see "Facer" and "Twitbook" as nothing more than the passing fad of egocentric, navel-gazing, less-than-20-somethings who want to make sure the world knows what they are doing every second of their lives. Yes, there is a lot of that out there. But the organizations that dismiss social media on this premise will find themselves on the dust heap of history.

The second are like lemmings. They see the rush to a new communication method, think there could be potential value, and run headlong over the ledge of technology to drown in an ocean they never expected. And it doesn't always have to be a headlong rush. Some organizations see others diving in, so they stick in a toe. However, that lemming's cliff is so steep and the waters so deep, the organizations' small foray quickly becomes a commitment and disaster that they weren't prepared for. And that is the tragedy of this second set of organizations. With just a little preparation, with just a few controls, that toe-dip of introduction could have led to great success.

Which leads us to the third and final type of organization. These are the ones who have seen the value of social media, who recognize the time is now, but have also taken a look at the real ramifications and taken the appropriate actions. Whether they dive in or stick in a toe, they are prepared (at least as prepared as anyone can be) for the rocks and shoals of the social media ocean.

So back to our original question: Why should anyone care about social media?

Because every participant in every organization has the opportunity to provide value by helping those organizations see the opportunities and risks related to social media. With a basic understanding of those opportunities and risks, any group can complete reviews that help ensure the organization's successful plunge into those waters.

What we are attempting to do in this book is help you help your organization to be in that third group—*organizations that see the value but understand the risks.* We are not going to be able to give you the specific answers on how to use social media within your organization. That is a broader subject for a different time. However, we provide the overview and tools you need to successfully partner with the business in achieving its social media goals.

CHAPTER 1

Social Media

An Overview

S ocial media has evolved from basic tools and Web sites used by professors and computer geeks into a behemoth that is fundamentally changing how people connect and converse with corporations, governments, traditional media, and each other. Until the advent of social media, organizations and traditional broadcast media had a stranglehold on the message. Most had the ability, and the desire, to ensure that communications were a simple monologue or, at the most, a very controlled two-way conversation. Without a widespread methodology for individuals to communicate information or opinions about an organization, commentary was limited to a small sphere of influence, mainly done through one-to-one communications—whether in person, on the phone, through the mail, or, more recently, via e-mail. While people would still get together and talk about political issues, brand name products, and their favorite meal at their local restaurant, the conversation was not scalable; it just simply had no way of reaching the masses.

The broader conversation was the job of the marketing and public relations teams. With sufficient resources, marketing could develop communications that could reach millions through television, radio, and print publications. At the same time, public relations professionals were garnering the attention of traditional media outlets, getting their message out through established news outlets. In both cases, the job focused on pushing messages to the audience and hoping the messages were compelling enough to create the desired outcome.

As time progressed through the mid- to late-1990s, the consumer's ability to go from one-to-one to one-to-few was empowering. People's ability to have a voice that could be heard beyond their immediate sphere of influence was beginning to grow. Through more advanced bulletin board systems, Internet forums, online chat, and personal Web sites, the ability for an individual's voice to reach the masses was about to become a reality. While organizations still resided in "monologue mode," there was the growing realization that this was becoming a trend that would have to be reckoned with in the near future.

For some organizations, this was exciting news. It meant that the small business could have a voice and gain ground on larger organizations with massive advertising budgets. For organizations that wanted to gain a closer connection to their customers, this meant there was now a way to listen and hear what was being said about their organization and products, start a conversation, and potentially develop meaningful relationships with stakeholders. However, for those who were happy controlling the message, this was going to mean a significant change in their overall communications strategy—a change that many did not want to make.

Today, social media has rapidly become part of how people communicate. Over the past seven or eight years, it has transformed from a way people pass time to a significant part of personal and corporate culture. This is especially true as broadband Internet access has become ubiquitous throughout the world. With the ability to instantly upload text, images, audio, and video content—and with the added dimension of immediate global access—traditional media methods have been distorted. This has empowered everyone to become a publisher, creating content and joining conversations regardless of the media format. While all of this opens up tremendous opportunities for businesses to grow closer to stakeholders, it also presents a brand new set of significant risks.

> Social media is like water. On its own, water does some cool things, but when combined with other compounds, it enabled the evolution of all forms of life. Social media on its own is nice, but when combined with other tools, it is enabling everything to evolve, from communications to business to politics to marketing.
>
> —Mike Volpe, VP Marketing, HubSpot

Definition of Social Media

There is no single recognized definition of social media. However, within the various descriptions that exist, it can be said that social media is the set of Web-based broadcast technologies that enable the democratization of content, giving people the ability to emerge from consumers of content to publishers. With the ability to achieve massive scalability in real time, these technologies empower people to connect with each other to create (or *co*-create) value through online conversation and collaboration.

It is important to note that the most significant outcome of applying these technologies is to help foster relationships with people. Whether it is as simple as helping families and friends stay connected or enabling a deeper connection with consumers, employees, vendors, and investors, the global power of these relationships is not only impressive but also evolving rapidly. It is also important that social media not be solely bundled within an IT framework. While there have been new technologies developed that helped facilitate these interactions, for the most part, they do not represent a sweeping change in the risks or auditing of the IT function.

History of Social Media

To gain insight into why social media is so popular and continues to rapidly evolve, it is important to look back and see how it has progressed over time. The following is a timeline of how Internet technologies began to embrace conversations and collaboration, from the early days of bulletin board systems to some of the latest trends in 2010. (We can't be held responsible for what happens from 2011 and beyond.)

1978–1989: The Conversation Begins—One-to-Few

Perhaps the first true social media tool was created back in 1978. The "Computerized Bulletin Board System" was the first form of communication that best meets the definition of social media. Developed by former IBM employee Ward Christensen, the value proposition was simple. Develop a program that would enable members of their community to post a message to others in the group. These were the typical messages about meeting times and locations, saving the community's organizers significant time in placing telephone calls. This was the first real case where an offline group used broadcast technologies to enable people to move beyond one-on-one conversation to "one-to-few." It also allowed for the democratization of their content, allowing members to post content as publishers and

6

deliver value through conversation and collaboration with other group members. While limited in scope, it was also a productive solution, especially considering that potentially dozens of phone calls would have to be made to convey the same message as a single post.

As the practicality of these bulletin boards grew, so did the functionality. While limited in bandwidth and typically not available to the average person, members of these "virtual communities" were able to engage in conversations, converse in message boards, access documents contributed by other community members, and so on. The electronic conversation was beginning.

1990–1994: User Adoption 1.0—The Internet Comes Alive

At the beginning of the 1990s, Internet access was primarily available to government, military, and academic organizations. It wasn't until 1993–1995 that access really opened up to everyone when Internet service providers (ISPs) began to offer services in most major U.S. cities. During this time, Prodigy and CompuServe emerged as the leaders, gaining critical mass in the commercial and in-home markets. In the mid-1990s, America Online (AOL) also gained significant popularity with consumers through aggressive advertising and the direct mailing of millions of CDs to consumers. These providers opened up the Internet to individuals through a more refined user interface that allowed them to participate in forums and develop and host basic Web sites.

While still rudimentary in nature, these exchanges were the first steps at a scalable social media solution. Though these services did not maintain their initial popularity, they can be attributed with enabling millions of commercial and home users the opportunity to enjoy their first interactive experiences—including the introduction of e-mail.

1995–1999: The Conversation Takes a Breath—The Dot-com Bubble

The period 1995 through 1999 saw an incredible boom in Web technologies (browsers, Web site design, etc.), e-commerce, and online ad serving (leading to the eventual bursting of the Internet bubble in early 2000). The vast majority of venture capital was applied to commerce and advertising-supported business models, resulting in less emphasis on the "next generations" of social media, and most business models remained with the traditional bulletin-board type application. Although this was a relatively slow period for the evolution of social media technologies, the changes occurring provided the springboard for events in the next century.

There were a few standouts that began to shape the future of social media. ICQ, an instant messaging system, was launched in 1996 and quickly acquired by AOL, eventually becoming the AIM platform in 1997 that is still popular today. Though most used it to only communicate with people they knew personally, it was the first mainstream application of using microformatted content—short packets of content—which is the backbone of the currently popular Twitter publishing platform. Created by users and spreading virally through the instant messaging community, abbreviations such as LOL and IMO have almost become a common part of our offline conversations. And, as much as we might like to, let's not forget emoticons either.☺

Another precursor for some of today's social media functionality was SixDegrees.com. Initially launched in 1997, the site was based on a "Web of Contacts" business model and allowed a user to establish a profile and connect with friends and family, building a virtual "six degrees of separation" community. It enabled some direct communication with the added ability to share connections with anyone else on the site.

SixDegrees.com was potentially ahead of its time, with site users complaining that there was little left to do after accepting "friend" requests, and most users were not interested in meeting strangers. It could not build a sustainable business model (especially during the bursting dot-com bubble) and the site eventually closed in 2000–2001. However, for the next generation of social media organizations, this experiment provided valuable guidance, showing that a true social media application not only supports the connectivity between its members but also allows them to become publishers of content, join in the conversation, and form relationships.

It was also in the late 1990s when blogging began to gain some traction after a very slow start. Initially used as personal diaries, it was during this time that the first organizations began developing hosted blogging tools. The first of many was Open Diary. Launching in 1998, it grew to include thousands of online diaries and was the first community to allow readers to comment on a blogger's post. This was quickly followed in 1999 with the launch of LiveJournal and the extremely popular Blogger, acquired by Google in 2003.

Though it might not seem like much, the ability to add comments was significant because it enabled an ongoing conversation to occur in a more relevant way than bulletin boards. As conversations grew, so did the popularity of the people publishing the content. This was also another key to helping individuals form relationships around a common interest or topic.

2000–2004: The Conversation Grows—One-to-Many

Social media site development really began to take off, both in terms of platform development and content creation, in 2000. This is also when user-generated content began reaching a level of critical mass, providing the first signal to organizations that people were able and willing to create content and join in conversations without organizational participation. While this had always been the case in the offline environment (as well as, to a small degree, online), it was this time when the volume of conversations reached a level where everyone was beginning to notice—and the conversations were becoming somewhat more interesting. While there wasn't a substantive understanding or response by most organizations, savvy communications professionals started to recognize the need to at least listen to what was being said about them and their competitors.

In early 2003, Friendster launched as the first social media platform that seemingly worked out most of the issues faced by its predecessors. Attracting 3 million users in the first six months, Friendster was positioned to dominate the social media platform space and is currently a leading platform in Asia with more than 115 million registered users. This was also the time when the phrase Web 2.0 began to catch on. As opposed to Web 1.0, which focused on centralized Web sites, this new era focused on the "Web as a platform" and was built around the collaborative creation of content and information sharing.

The year 2003 also marked the launch of another well-known platform—LinkedIn. This social networking platform enabled professional colleagues to connect and collaborate together and in groups. It was not only an important communication tool for employees but also for human resource professionals who were looking to recruit new talent. While it took some time to gain momentum, by 2010 LinkedIn claimed to have more than 50 million users, with more than 50 percent located outside the United States.

Another platform that launched in 2003 was Wordpress. This tool allowed individuals who had no programming knowledge to start a blog in minutes and gave people the choice of either downloading the software or using a free hosted solution. Wordpress helped lead the shift in the adoption of user-generated content and "citizen journalism." What set Wordpress apart from other platforms was that users could host a blog on their own domain and have much greater control over the usability and design aspects of their sites. Additionally, Wordpress was launched as an open source tool, allowing third-party developers to continually enhance the platform through the development of onscreen tools that are embedded into a Web page—also known as widgets (finally, a widget is no longer a fictional product!). These widgets provided users with significantly greater control and functionality of their sites. Today, a number of the most highly trafficked sites run on the Wordpress platform.

The year 2003 also saw the advent of social bookmarking with the launch of the Web site del.icio.us (now simply delicious.com). This gave users the ability to bookmark a Web page using freely chosen keywords or "tags," creating a user-generated *folksonomy* (basically a user-generated taxonomy around a particular topic). The differentiator between bookmarking and file sharing is that the data is not stored, but a simple link to the Web page is provided, allowing the user to access the information later. These links can be saved privately, shared within select groups, or made public, allowing users to search through the bookmarks by popularity, category, tag, or date.

While social bookmarking helped people find the content they wanted to save, real simple syndication (RSS) made it easier for content updates such as blog posts, news headlines, audio, video, and so on to be published and distributed in a standardized format. Though it originated in 1997, the current version (RSS 2.0) was developed by Dave Winer, founder of UserLand software. This version was made available in 2003 by the Berkman Center for Internet & Society at Harvard Law School. A typical "feed" will include either the full or summarized text with

11

additional data on author and date. What makes RSS so important is it allows anyone to quickly listen and gather content from a particular publisher. This provides an efficient method of monitoring news and streamlines communication between publishers and readers.

However, the biggest launch in 2003 came in August with MySpace. In what became the most popular online social networking site, MySpace offered users a greater level of on-page control, empowering them to be more self-expressive in how their content was displayed and consumed. This quickly became a popular feature and a significant differentiator from Friendster, catching the attention of everyone from musicians and celebrities to teenagers and major corporations. As adoption grew, having a MySpace page was considered an indication that an organization wanted to have a communications strategy that connected to a younger, hipper audience. It also caught the attention of political candidates and CEOs who wanted to be seen as being in touch with current trends.

Though MySpace has lost some of its popularity, it is still a heavily trafficked Web site and a powerful source of personal communications. The extensive use of this and other sites by employees caused many corporate IT departments to block access because it was impacting workplace productivity and serving as a potential source to leak confidential internal information.

The year 2004 kicked off with the launch of Flickr, a photo-sharing site, which quickly grew to include billions of pages of photos, videos, and community content. Flickr provides a robust community for another form of publisher—the photographer/videographer. With both amateurs and professionals sharing images, tips, and information on photography, the site successfully leverages the aspects of content, contacts, and conversation as a basis to form relationships based on a mutual interest.

The growth of social media platforms did not slow down during 2004. In April of that year, Facebook was launched on the Harvard University campus with the initial intent of offering a platform for students to interact. Under the initial domain thefacebook.com, the Harvard networking site grew quickly, leading to expansion on other university campuses, including Stanford, Columbia, and Yale. Expanding to high school students helped propel the next level of expansion in 2005, and, by September 2006, the site (now Facebook.com) was available to everyone. With a cleaner, more refined user interface, Facebook was the answer for many MySpacers who were frustrated with confusing, ad-laden page layouts. By the end of 2006, Facebook had 12 million users. According to Facebook, this number has grown to more than 500 million active users.

Beyond the design elements offered (or not offered), what has made Facebook addictive is a combination of instant status updates with third-party social games and applications. The status updates allow users to quickly scan the activities and events of their friends, and the social gaming applications create a somewhat addictive environment that increases both time on site as well as interactivity among users.

Facebook's success can also be attributed to the more mature nature of its audience. As opposed to some sites that tend to attract a younger demographic, more than 60 percent of Facebook users are over the age of 35. According to a 2010 survey by Royal Pingdom, social games also appeal to an older, more female demographic with the largest single group being 35 to 44 years old. For organizations, this provides a significant opportunity for listening to, engaging with, and building close relationships with their stakeholders.

While certainly not the powerhouse of Facebook, Yelp, a tool for local searches and consumer reviews, successfully launched in October 2004. By combining the qualities of social networking with a robust user review process for local businesses, Yelp stands out as an innovator for drawing attention to the small to midsized businesses. Users benefit by being able to log in, enter a location (city, ZIP code, etc.), along with such terms as "pizza" or "dry cleaners," and discover all the businesses in the area that meet that criteria. Combined with reviews, users can ideally find the best option as determined by the community. For organizations, Yelp is a powerful relationship management tool for listening to their customers. This feedback can be invaluable for thanking happy customers for their business, reading positive comments, and responding to or assisting customers who did not have a positive experience. By 2010, this young start-up had grown into a social media powerhouse, serving more than 30 million active users per month.

2005–2009: User Adoption 2.0—The Conversation Comes Alive

If 2000–2004 was about building platforms and tools, 2005–2009 could be defined as the period of user adoption and the remarkable change in how users connect, converse, and build relationships.

There were major advances in social media tools and technologies that spurred adoption. The first occurred in May 2005 with the launch of YouTube, the video-sharing Web site. Before its public launch, there were not many avenues for the average Internet user to share video. Part of the issue was the availability of broadband Internet access. The other was a lack of online storage. YouTube solved both of these issues and combined it with a simple user interface, overnight empowering virtually anyone to become a publisher of video content.

The second major platform came in 2006 when Twitter was launched (or "hatched" in the sense that their logo is a bluebird). Twitter is positioned as a microblogging (or microformat) method to publish content, and it took some time to gain traction in the marketplace. With a maximum of 140 characters, "tweeting" became an easy form of content publishing that allowed individuals to "follow" other people and

14

provide status updates and information in short bursts. Users, known as "tweeters," can also embed links within their message. By using link-shortening services such as bit.ly, a long Web address can effectively be shortened to just a few characters. While the Twitter platform is interesting, the bigger movement comes from the popularity of the "status update," enabling individuals the ability to create, share, and converse using shorter forms of content. As Facebook emerged from the college campuses and became available to the general public, combined with the launch of Twitter and the ability to send a text message from a mobile device, social media started to shift from long-form content found in blogs to this shorter form.

Today, Twitter is one of the most powerful tools an organization has to listen to conversations that are happening in real time (search.twitter.com). Many are also finding it to be an invaluable tool for customer service (Best Buy's @Twelpforce) as well as a powerful revenue driver (Dell's @DellOutlet).

The third advance came more as a technology innovation than a particular platform. In 2008, shortly after the release of the iPhone 3G, the App Store was introduced along with the ability for third-party developers to create mobile applications. These applications came in many forms, from games to productivity enhancements to social networking tools. Now available in most smart phones, these applications bring the Internet to the mobile device, creating new and interesting ways to connect, converse, and build relationships. It not only enables more people to participate in social media, but also facilitates the expansion of microformat content creation.

2010 and Beyond—The Launch of the Statusphere

The trend away from blogs and static Web pages continues to grow into 2010, as the term *blogosphere* begins to fade and *statusphere* begins to emerge. While there is still interest in blogs, the sharing of opinions, and the desire to participate in online conversations, content creation is moving away from "what I think" to "what is happening right now." The major accelerant to this shift is based on the global positioning system (GPS) found within smart phones. As developers began to uncover new consumer applications for GPS technology, *location-based services* (LBS) began to emerge, with the intent of unlocking the mobile experience to its full potential. LBS applications essentially allow people to identify their location using the mobile GPS functionality and "check in" at locations. This check-in can be shared through social networks and be seen by their friends. One such service, Foursquare (which launched in 2009), was created as both an LBS social networking site and a mobile gaming application that would allow users to become the "mayor" of locations they frequented as well as earning badges for certain activities or levels of participation. Retailers such as Starbucks have created incentives for their "mayors," allowing them to receive discounts or free products upon each check-in.

While the concept of the check-in combined with a real-time status update can be a viable method of social networking, individual privacy concerns have risen, primarily among women who do not want to disclose their location to potential strangers. This concept has been dubbed "locational privacy." Sites such as PleaseRobMe.com were launched as awareness tools to stress the risks of oversharing locations through social networks.

A Minefield of Opportunities and Risks

What began as a way for a few dozen members of a select group to effectively communicate with each other has evolved into a global phenomenon and a major cultural shift in how people connect and communicate. With the recognition that everyone is, or at least can be, a publisher, the organizational implications are tremendous. While this means the organization is no longer in complete control of its message, the good news is that it has the ability to develop stronger and more meaningful relationships with stakeholders, creating an opportunity to provide much greater value. Through effective listening, connecting, and conversing with stakeholders, organizations can gain a greater understanding of those stakeholder needs. Starting with message forums and connecting with friends, social media has evolved into a diverse set of tools and technologies that enables organizations to communicate with customers in real time based on their exact location. These tools and technologies also enable organizations to "crowdsource" (outsourcing tasks or projects to large groups of people such as customers or vendors), creating everything from new products to television commercials.

At the same time, with opportunity comes risk. To date, the majority of organizations have not addressed the risk of social media. According to the Deloitte LLP 2009 Ethics & Workplace Survey, titled *Social Networking and Reputational Risk in the Workplace,* 58 percent of corporate executives agree that the reputational risks that can arise from self-expression through social networking should be a boardroom discussion. However, only 15 percent are actively addressing the issue. More surprising, only 17 percent have formal programs in place to monitor and mitigate the potential reputational risks related to the use of social networks. Additionally, the study cited that only 22 percent of respondents say that their organization has a formal policy to dictate how employees can use social networking tools.

So beyond cool online tools and mass consumer adoption, where is the value for an organization?

It's in relationships. It's the ability to move beyond the monologue (and monolithic) way of controlled communications and embrace an open and honest dialogue. When social media is implemented effectively, it provides a scalable method to foster trust between the organization and the stakeholder to work collectively for mutual gain.

A great example of the value that social media and relationships can bring to an organization can be found in the foreword of Geoffrey Moore's bestseller *Crossing the Chasm* (HarperBusiness, 1991). As Regis McKenna writes:

> Fundamentally, marketing must refocus away from selling product and toward creating relationships. Customers don't like to be "owned" if that implies lack of choice or freedom. But they do like to be "owned" if what that means is a vendor taking ongoing responsibility for the success of their joint ventures. Ownership in this sense means an abiding commitment and a strong sense of mutuality in the development of the marketplace. When customers encounter this kind of ownership, they tend to become fanatically loyal to their supplier, which in turn builds a stable economic base for profitability and growth.

While the history and evolution of social media can sometimes seem as though it is merely a set of tools for people to share their favorite recipes, chat online, or look up old high school friends, it has actually become a corporate imperative requiring both a strategic approach as part of a communications plan in addition to the tactical implementation and tracking with the right metrics. With processes and policies built around traditional communications processes that have been in place for decades, a comprehensive review must be conducted to ensure that the organization has the adequate governance, risk, and control measures in place to capitalize on these opportunities while protecting it from excessive risk.

CHAPTER 2

Social Media

A Corporate Strategy

Social media is quickly becoming a part of mainstream business practice. Organizations are beginning to learn and understand that it's not just about having Facebook fans, but that it can lead to significant strategic value. While this is intriguing, making it actually pay off within an organization still eludes many corporate executives. This was supported by a 2009 study by Russell Herder and Ethos Business Law, indicating that 51 percent of executives do not use social media because they do not know enough about it. In addition, 81 percent believe that social media can be a security risk to the organization and fear it could not only be detrimental to employee productivity but also damage the organization's reputation. Despite these concerns, the respondents also acknowledge that there is value and that, overall, social media cannot be ignored. In fact, 81 percent believe that social media can enhance relationships with customers/clients and build brand reputation, with almost 70 percent believing it can be valuable in the recruitment process and serve as a customer service tool (64 percent).

What is the reason for the opposing points of view? One is that most social media strategies (or the lack thereof) are not strategic, focusing more on the tools and tactics than on the relationships and business objectives. To build the business case for social media, only a comprehensive strategy aligned to business objectives combined with policies and procedures that mitigate risk will be able to properly demonstrate value while calming fears. As discussed in Chapter 1, the value to an organization is the ability to build real relationships with real people; it is not about the tools and technologies. Building deeper relationships with stakeholders should be part of an overall organizational strategy with social media helping achieve its success. It is through the effective use of social media that an organization can build the right relationships with the right people to realize value.

Another challenge with the adoption of social media (especially at the executive level) is how it is treated in the workplace. For some, it is a compliance issue, making sure employees are not spending a couple of hours a day playing Farmville or Mafia Wars (no offense to Zynga on this one— your games can be addicting). In this case, social media strategies are about compliance and enforcement, not engagement. This approach effectively ignores how the organization can use social media to drive business performance.

The vast difference between seeing social media as a compliance issue or a driver of business performance often leaves executives and staff confused in trying to develop the right balance. Because of these issues, we spend a significant amount of time in this chapter on how to develop an effective and comprehensive social media strategy. We want to emphasize this topic because most organizations do not have such a strategy. In most cases, social media has become a tactical event based on the use of tools, creating a misunderstanding of the value of social media and leading to an increased risk for the organization. At the same time, this presents an excellent opportunity for internal auditing to partner with others in the organization, serving as independent consultants who can help provide a social media strategy framework that aligns with business objectives.

Delivering Value: If Nothing Else—Listen and Learn

There's an interesting misconception that some people have about social media—that the organization has the ability to somehow prohibit or opt out of social media altogether. This mind-set suggests that, because the organization has decided not to participate in social media, its customers won't talk about the products or services, employees won't talk to their friends about work, and the world will sit back and wait for the organization to speak to it. Unfortunately, that is old-school thinking. The organization, no matter how much it longs for the good old days, is no longer in control of the conversation. Further, the failure to use (or actually prohibit the use of) social media as a way to listen to customers and their conversations is simply naive. This basically sends a message that the organization doesn't care about its stakeholders and that, if they want to engage with the organization, they will have to do it on the organization's terms. In this day, when social media is used by more than 80 percent of adults in the United States, failure to use social media channels to listen to stakeholders (and competitors) can subject the organization to unnecessary reputational risk.

The bottom line is that it is not if the organization is going to participate in social media, it is to what extent it will participate. The important thing to note is that just because your organization has made the decision to prohibit the use of social media internally don't be foolish enough to think that prohibits your stakeholders from using it to talk about the organization.

The encouraging aspect here is that a commitment to continual listening and learning can yield tremendous results with little investment. Stakeholders are out there using social networks to talk about your organization, products, competitors, community, and staff. They can suggest enhancements to products, suggest new store locations or hours of operation, provide feedback on Web site functionality, and so on. They are telling the organization about themselves and what they want. These insights are extremely valuable.

There are also numerous tools to help you listen effectively, from free online tools that have basic functionality to more elaborate systems that measure the overall sentiment and influence of the conversations (an extensive list is provided in Appendix C). If you find that you are conducting an audit of the social media activities and no one is effectively listening, then the rest of the audit will be interesting to say the least (and there is a pretty good chance that you will hear "We got this video and we're going to get it to go viral!" somewhere in the conversation).

Delivering Value: The Social Media Strategy

Interestingly, one of the more significant elements missing from a social media strategy can be the strategy itself. It is important to not just accept a document as being a strategic plan but to ensure that the plan is more than a list of social media tools that will be deployed with goals for increasing the number of friends, followers, and page views. That's tactical and, while there is a place for this, it is not a part of the strategic plan. Strategic planning is hard work and oftentimes social media has been left to mid- or lower-level staff that might not have an adequate level of insight into the overall organizational strategy and business objectives.

24

The Evolution of Social Media Strategy

The first in the evolution is the *add-on strategy*. Though it is popular and fairly easy to develop, it fails in that it is more about the technology than the relationships. In other words, it is really not a strategy at all. In this case, the organization adopts a tool (blog, Facebook, Twitter, etc.), but does nothing else internally. This is easy to identify as you will hear something like "We have a Facebook strategy." That's not a strategy; it is a tactical plan disguised to look like a strategy.

> Discipline and process are critical to the success of any social media strategy.
>
> —Kelly Feller, Intel

The second is the mandated strategy. In this case, it assumes that social media is interchangeable with existing processes. This will take on the appearance of swapping out one technology for a social media technology. For example, all e-mail newsletters will be replaced by blogs with the same content. This makes the assumption that the social media tool is the latest and greatest thing and that e-mail is old school or ineffective. Again, the focus is on the technologies, not the relationships. A mandated strategy comes close to falling under the "shiny object syndrome" and will often resemble the "We have a Facebook strategy" comment above. (Sorry, Mark Zuckerberg, nothing personal. Facebook is an amazing social technology.)

The third is a "real" strategic plan. It recognizes that the purpose of social media is to develop relationships and use the appropriate social technologies to leverage connections and conversations between real people, and it involves a new level of commitment to learning and collaboration. A true social media strategy has the greatest ability to support the achievement of business objectives.

Developing the Strategy

In this section, a number of factors are discussed that either determine the strategy or should be included in an effective strategic plan.

Are the Current Social Media Activities Currently in the "Experimental Phase"?

Experimenting is okay and most likely the best way to start, so long as everyone understands that these are experiments (or it could be viewed as a series of incremental successes and failures). It doesn't mean that the activities should not be aligned with the business objectives, but just that there might be less formality to the overall function in terms of scope and resources. In some ways, organizations that are hesitant to engage in social media might be best served by a series of small but focused tests to determine to what extent these activities should become a permanent part of the business operations.

According to Bonin Bough, global director of Digital and Social Media for PepsiCo, the real social media goal at Pepsi was less about the big strategy and more about the experimentation and getting the small wins. Dell is another example of a company that initially approached social media by implementing pilot programs composed of small tests that delivered a quick proof of concept, enabling the company to quickly determine where the best opportunities and challenges exist. While there is an inherent risk in undergoing these programs, experimentation can limit the risk exposure and get everyone working together in a collaborative fashion. This approach also does not overpromise and underdeliver. By using a series of small wins and constant learning, it is easier to prove the value of relationship building using social technologies that drive business results. A series of tactical activities will make it challenging to experience small wins and prove the case, but strategic experimentation can pay off, fostering a greater commitment to learning. However, don't forget that this doesn't mean the experiments should be done without a strategy, or at least a well-defined plan that considers both the opportunities and risks.

Clear Alignment between the Social Strategy and the Business Objectives

Do the organization's objectives include obtaining a better understanding of the customers, increasing customer retention and loyalty, driving product innovation, improving service, or increasing reliability? If so, then the social media strategy should clearly state the connection between the strategy and these business goals. For example, if the business goal is to improve customer service, the social media strategy should clearly show a direct correlation to that goal. When properly aligned, business objectives help guide the best use of social media tactics to deliver value.

The organization's approach to social media can support a number of different functions within the business and it is easy to get lost in developing a great strategy that does not help drive the business. For example, marketing can develop a great strategy to use social media to grow market share. However, if the organization's primary goal is to improve customer satisfaction by, say, 20 percent, success for the marketing department can come at the cost of the organization's objectives. This is another reason why executives often struggle with buying into the value of social media—they might see value, but it might not be in the area that really matters at the time.

It is also important that the overall strategy have a methodology for measuring effectiveness through relevant metrics. As social media adoption begins to grow, there can be significant disruption within the structure of the organization, meaning that major decisions need to be made with metrics. It is vital to understand not only the measurements of activity (such as the number of fans, followers, or comments) but also the outcomes and value they bring to the business. While these are discussed further in this chapter, it is important to ensure the strategy includes appropriate metrics and that they are aligned to achieve business goals.

One last note: If the organization has not clearly articulated its business objectives and operates more tactically, then it is virtually impossible to have a successful social media strategy. In this case, the best advice might be to stay in an experimental phase and identify a couple of departmental goals that can lead to incremental success and learning. During this period, avoid investing significant resources until these objectives have been identified and a proper alignment is achieved.

Social Media Strategy as Part of the Existing Strategy

Ideally, a social media strategy is not a stand-alone document and is actually an element added into an existing strategic plan. This is important because social media can touch so many current operations of a business and, when properly executed, is about integration and collaboration within an organization. Social media strategies that are developed in a stand-alone environment tend to operate in a silo—almost the exact opposite of the original intended purpose, and generally lead to a network of uncoordinated tactical initiatives that organically spread throughout the organization from one silo to another. In particular, a silo approach to social media strategy can affect such areas as accountability in the organization;

consistent communication to various stakeholders; coordination of messaging; and staffing, training, technical resources, and budgeting issues.

If the activities are still experimental and the scope was communicated effectively, this might not be a significant issue until there is a long-term commitment. However, once there is a commitment to engaging stakeholders through social media, strategic planning and prioritization must occur.

A well-constructed strategy will also include a planned migration into various departments based on the overarching business objectives. A strategic plan that overreaches and is committed to serving too many business units or stakeholder groups at one time runs significant risks with the execution, staffing, and funding of these programs. Beyond listening, a key ingredient for success in any social media activity is consistency. If the organization attempts to extend the activities too quickly, the risk of not serving each stakeholder group consistently increases.

Identify the Target Audiences and How Each Uses Social Media

Here's where it starts to get a little more interesting. With numerous stakeholders and just as many (if not more) ways to engage, knowing who you want to engage is vitally important. This is also where many organizations go astray and head straight to tactics. Even if you go along with the belief that "everyone is doing it," that doesn't mean that every stakeholder has a Twitter handle (user name) or, if they do, that they want to engage with the organization in that manner. Thinking that social media tools are ubiquitous and one channel fits all is a misguided strategy (a "fail" for Twitter addicts).

An effective social media strategy should not only include specific details about the target audience but also the desired relationship or conversational engagement, combined with what that target audience is ready for and how they typically use social media. By understanding the organization's target audience, as well as how they use social media, it becomes easier to develop a strategy that engages the right people in the right place at the right time. It also enables the strategic plan to identify the best ways to converse and build relationships in the most relevant manner.

In 2007, Charlene Li and Josh Bernoff, working together at Forrester Research, came up with Social Technographics, a process that identified categories of how people use social media. According to the January 2010 update of Social Technographics, there are seven categories of participation. These categories are not exclusive and people may participate in more than one category at any given time.

- **Creators**. People who publish blogs, develop images, create video content, host podcasts, and so on.
- **Conversationalists**. People who provide status updates in sites like Twitter.
- **Critics**. People who provide reviews and comments on blogs and forums.
- **Collectors**. People who vote on and tag articles and other content on sites like delicious.com.
- **Joiners**. People who join larger social networking sites such as Facebook and LinkedIn and create profiles.
- **Spectators**. People who are more passive, but enjoy reading, watching, and listening to social media that has been developed by creators, conversationalists, and critics.
- **Inactives**. People who do not participate in any form of social media.

Taking this information into account, it becomes easier to determine whether the strategy is positioned for success. For example, if the business objective is to increase brand awareness and perception among C-level executives, it is important to determine how these executives are engaging in social media and what forms they are willing to use to build relationships with the organization. (This is an example where well-executed experiments can help ensure the right approach is being used.) Without this level of insight, the organization runs the risk of trying to engage with people who are not listening. (If a post is entered into a blog and no one is listening, has any point been made?)

Worse, the message might go through a channel where other stakeholders are congregating, but have no interest in that particular topic. Again, this behavior demonstrates to stakeholders that the organization does not understand (or potentially care) about who they are and what they need, thereby creating a new level of reputational risk.

The other benefit of understanding how the target audience wants to build a relationship is gaining an understanding of the conversational style that will best resonate with the audience in an authentic way. By the way, just saying that the conversations will "be authentic" doesn't cut it either. It is very easy to be authentic and well meaning and still disenfranchise your audience. Part of an effective social media strategy is understating which conversational style is applied to each stakeholder group. In some instances, the tone may need to be more serious, reflecting safety and assurance (e.g., crisis communications, financial reporting, etc.). Others can be quirky and fun (e.g., internal communications, consumer engagement, etc.). Both can be authentic, but the conversational style will be different. Just because it is social media doesn't mean that the end state is always relaxed and informal. A significant mismatch in conversational styles from the stakeholder's perception could lead to a negative experience. That's all part of being authentic.

The Social Media Plan

After assessing the strategy, there should also be a supporting plan that outlines specific applications of social media within the business (e.g., customer service) as well as the specific goals, the social media channels that will be used, the level and types of engagement, and who is responsible for these activities. Similar to the strategic plan for social media, it is important that the implementation plan is also not a stand-alone document. It should be incorporated into other plans within the organization.

Goals

Goals are unique to the applications and the organization itself and should support the organizational goals. Very often, they include reference to the metrics established to show the success of the organization's move toward social media.

In many cases, the social media plans contain goals that are simply based on areas like an increase in fans or followers. It is only through understanding the value of a fan or follower, as well as how these individuals impact the organization's goals, that the true value of the activity can be recognized.

Channels

This part of the plan gets into specifics, identifying the various social media channels that will be used. For example, the customer service team might use Twitter as the channel of preference to increase inquiry response time by 20 percent, whereas enhancing the brand awareness and perception might include having a Facebook page, uploading video, and starting a company blog.

A comprehensive plan will also detail the specific tools within each channel that will be used. This helps identify any costs that will be incurred as well as any risks or incompatibilities from an IT perspective. It will also indicate the level of training required to ensure the staff is well versed in the use of these tools. From the previous example, customer service might choose to use CoTweet, a specific tool that enables enterprise-wide Twitter account management, and the company blog will be delivered using Wordpress and hosted on a subdomain from the organization's primary Web site (blog.abccompany.com). There are many instances when this might seem trivial, but there are implications with the various channels that need to be taken into account. Using the wrong channel or the wrong tool has the potential to expose the organization to additional reputational and security risks. If nothing else, defining the channels makes sure that all parties involved in social media understand not only what is being used, but why.

Engagement

Engagement is at the heart of relationship building with the stakeholder and can really make or break the success of the program. Engagement sets forth the promise made to the stakeholder in terms of the value that will be delivered; how it will be delivered; and the expectations for frequency, response time, etc. In a sense, the level of engagement is the service-level agreement between the organization and the stakeholder.

The strategic plan should already provide an understanding of the target audience, where they congregate, how they will be most receptive to the organization's message, and the conversational style that is most likely to foster a strong relationship. From that, the plan should include specifics on the level of engagement. For example, the plan should outline whether social media will be used to listen, share information, comment on other content, or create original content such as a blog post or podcast.

The plan should also include the frequency of that content. Consistency is the main point here. The sporadic use of social media in the channel, the timing, and form of engagement will set the tone for building relationships and delivering results. Going back to the customer service example, if the goal is to increase inquiry response time using Twitter as the communications tool (aligned with the overall strategy), then the plan should specify the response time goal and the "hours of operation." Even though Twitter is a 24/7 platform, it might not be realistic to have a customer service member handling inquires on that same time frame. However, it is important to clearly communicate this to the stakeholders so the proper expectation is set.

It is also important to note that just because you can, doesn't mean you should. A proper social media plan acknowledges the limits of the organization. While there are many tools that can be used, some do not align with the strategy, and, even if they do, resources (both financial and human) are limited. It is much better to do a few things very well than to attempt to engage across many channels haphazardly. While some organizations have dedicated teams that thrive on high levels of engagement across numerous channels, many others are successfully using social media with a low frequency of engagement using just a few channels.

Staffing and Funding

"Social media is free!" is a myth that has been circulating for years—and it's a big one. While it is true most of the tools are available to the general public at no cost, it does not mean the organization should not devote resources to the social media activity. Even at a very basic listening level (using free tools), there is some labor component that needs to be allocated. This is especially true when a social media program is part of achieving an organizational goal. In the customer service example, each team member needs to be properly trained and coached on the use of Twitter in resolving customer service inquiries. They should not only understand the audience they will be conversing with but also the conversational style and service-level agreement for response time. For some people, this will be a new and potentially uncomfortable communication tool and will not come naturally. This activity also needs to be supervised with adequate reporting to determine whether the goal is being met. There might also be a financial commitment in the use of software as well as the potential integration with other customer relationship management or customer service platforms.

Metrics

A proper social media plan should also include the relevant metrics that support the goals as well as those that support the overall social media initiative. Chapter 3 provides an in-depth overview of social media metrics.

Social Media Policies

According to the Russell Herder and Ethos Business Law study, 69 percent of respondents said that their organization does not have formal policies that dictate how employees can use social networking tools. Though much of social media is about empowerment and letting go of the message, that doesn't mean that there should not be "rules of engagement" spelling out what is acceptable and what is not. While it might be perfectly acceptable to "friend" a client or vendor within a corporate environment, it certainly isn't acceptable for a grade school teacher to "friend" his or her students. This was reiterated by Joshua-Michele Ross in a 2009 *Forbes* article: ". . . if you think [social media guidelines] don't apply to you, you are probably already on the endangered species list." Chapter 4 provides additional information on social media policies.

Applying Social Media to Achieve Business Objectives

Success will ultimately come from applying social media activities to the right business objectives. Some of the more popular applications of social media are being used to address:

- Increasing revenue
- Improving customer satisfaction and loyalty
- Recruiting and retaining the best talent
- Product development and innovation
- Enhancing brand awareness and perception

There are some outstanding practical examples of some of these. By exploring how each delivered on an effective strategy and plan, it will become easier for the auditor to assess how these can be successfully applied to various business units within an organization. While some of the following examples represent larger consumer brands, the application and scalability can be applied to organizations and industries of varying sizes.

Increasing Revenue

To drive sales, Dell has created a tremendous following of more than 1.5 million followers on Twitter and is driving millions of dollars in annual revenue through this channel. They were successful because they listened and learned from their audience and understood that people were searching social networks such as Twitter to find specials and sales on computers and consumer electronics. They also understood that they would have to engage in proactive dialogues and appeal primarily to conversationalists (through status updates on Twitter and Facebook). This was not a "Twitter" strategy, but most likely a subset of an e-commerce strategy using social networks to help increase revenue for the Dell Outlet. In accomplishing this objective, they have done a number of things well.

Humanized the Brand   Dell humanized the company by identifying who at Dell was conversing with the audience via Twitter. Dell put a real person into the conversation—Stefanie Nelson—and invited people to comment and ask questions directly to Stefanie at @StefanieAtDell.

Reduced Organizational Risk   Dell is effective at using @DellOutlet as the main account for that business line, while using @StefanieAtDell for Dell business on an individual level. This allows Stefanie to maintain @StefanieAtDell no matter her role with the company, while allowing someone else to manage @DellOutlet sometime in the future, if necessary. This helps reduce the risk if the person used their individual name @StefanieNelson (should Stefanie leave the organization, so do 1.5 million in followers and the revenue) or force an awkward transition if @StefanieAtDell has to become @DavidAtDell.

Adopted the Appropriate Conversational Style   Dell (through Stefanie) has adopted the right conversational style for its customers and the social technology. @DellOutlet is not just about promoting sales; it is about building a relationship with the customer while promoting items on sale. For these conversations, Stefanie is conversational and proactive in the way she builds relationships with customers and prospective customers.

Expectations Were Set   If someone inadvertently stumbles onto @DellOutlet, they quickly learn that not only is Stefanie managing this account, but it is specifically there for U.S. sales of refurbished Dell computers and electronics. It is also clear that more Dell Twitter accounts can be found at Dell.com/Twitter. This helps consumers avoid the ambiguity of "Is this the right place for me?" It is also apparent through the conversations that, even if someone has arrived at the wrong location, Stefanie will direct the person to the right area. She is not the one to manage issues to resolution (that's not her job), but she will provide assistance. This methodology reduces reputational risk by proactively helping customers locate the place to find the right answer.

They Trust   It is time to end this example on a high note. Dell trusts its employees to do the right thing. Trust is built on a foundation of knowledge, training, organizational structure, performance, and the ability to monitor activity (trust, but verify). What works is providing the staff involved in social media with an understanding of the strategy and the metrics used to assess performance boundaries, as well as the tools and training needed to effectively perform the job.

While it is reckless to say "You are in charge of social media, so I trust that whatever you say is appropriate," it is just as reckless to have a policy that says every post, update, and the like has to be reviewed by corporate communications and legal. It is important to understand the potential opportunity cost when certain staff is not trusted with the ability to develop relationships with stakeholders using social technologies. Customers want to talk to people; they want to talk with Stefanie, not an aggregation of Stefanie, the vice president of corporate communications, and legal counsel, who will, most likely, beat any form of personality out to best mitigate risk while positioning the organization's key messages.

Improving Customer Satisfaction and Loyalty   This is another area that is often at the top of the list in organizations. Why? Because when stakeholders begin talking about a brand, it is often related to customer satisfaction—both positive and negative. Though the situation can be amplified with a bad experience, customers are also eager to share experiences with brands they love. Nothing says "You had me at hello" like an organization that reaches out to build a relationship by thanking the customer. Similarly, many bad (or potentially bad) experiences can be avoided or reversed when the organization is actively listening and engaging with customers—sending the message "Help me to help you" and really meaning it. (Sorry for the repetitive *Jerry Maguire* lines, but they just work here.)

Microsoft's Most Valuable Professional (MVP) program embraces their audience by rewarding some of their most loyal and passionate supporters. With approximately 4,000 MVPs from 90 countries serving 90 Microsoft technologies, their reach is beyond impressive. The honor that many of these individuals have in being part of this program shows up on social networking profiles, pictures, blog posts, videos, e-mail signatures, and so forth. While they do not receive cash compensation, there is a material connection as they often receive free products, early access to new versions, conference admission, and so on.

So what does Microsoft get out of the program? According to its Web site, more than 10 million questions per year. This is an excellent form of customer-supported customer service. By being hand-selected, MVPs are well vetted for their expertise and professionalism, as well as trusted to provide authentic assistance to the greater technology community. Additionally, the cost reduction related to staffing and training such a diverse workforce is almost impossible to imagine. Again, an organization doesn't stumble onto this by accident. This is a deliberate, strategic initiative that incorporates social technologies and passionate creators to provide global customer service to its users. It serves as an excellent example of how listening to target audiences and discovering how that audience wants to build a relationship with an organization can advance a business objective.

Recruiting and Retaining the Best Talent

There is a tendency for organizations to only adopt social media for external audiences. However, it is important to recognize the benefits of applying these strategies internally as well. Empowering employees to become advocates for the organization can serve not only as a motivator and employee retention tool but can also assist in recruiting new talent.

One of the best examples of using social media for recruiting and retaining the best talent is at Sodexo. To reach their large and diverse workforce and to be effective at an enterprise level, they had to develop a strategy that addressed a number of distinct audiences with different conversational styles. In planning their use of social media, they also had to identify which channels would be used as well as what level of engagement was appropriate. When reviewing the Sodexo Web site, it is apparent that the use of social media is being directly aligned with its organizational strategy and business goals, and that it is based on a high level of engagement using numerous channels.

Sodexo also understood that this initiative would die if left in a human resources silo. The company empowered its employees (including former employees) to build personal relationships and create a common place for prospective employees to directly engage with the brand in a manner in which all participants felt comfortable. Empowering employees to engage directly with candidates can build stronger and more relevant relationships. Not only did these activities result in increased activity to the site, but it also allowed Sodexo to reduce its recruitment advertising expenses by $300,000 in 2009.

Product Development and Innovation

Product innovation takes on a whole new angle when combined with social media. This blending of product innovation and social media can take many forms, from something as simple as a product innovation contest, to something as complicated as a private skunk works operation combining staff, vendors, customers (current, past, and prospective), academics, and even competitors to come together in a virtual environment to solve very complex problems. The thought leaders are the organizations that are seeking feedback to help keep the organization ahead of the curve. In most instances, these participants are critics, creators, and conversationalists, all with the desire to participate and tell it like it is. Yes, people will go online and criticize the organization, but at least they are trying to help the organization improve. If they didn't care, they would just rant rather than suggest. However, failure to acknowledge and engage these people can alienate them more than if they just went on a rant. This requires a further commitment to developing relationships and authentically engaging the audience to help spur the most viable product innovations. It probably won't be long before failing to solicit and recognize consumer-created suggestions and innovations will leave an organization seeming arrogant, irrelevant, and out of touch.

Starbucks is a great example of how to embrace customers for the betterment of the business. Instead of living within the four walls of the corporation, Starbucks launched MyStarbucksIdea.com and invited the masses to contribute ideas on how to make the Starbucks experience even better. Ideas can come in the form of products, experiences, or involvement (community and corporate social responsibility). Starbucks is completely transparent with the ideas submitted, encouraging conversation to occur around these ideas, including the status of each idea. They also encourage participation at the employee level, empowering associates throughout the organization to engage and discuss the proposed ideas.

It also worth pointing out that this Web site is powered by Salesforce.com, allowing Starbucks to record, track, and manage each inquiry from each contributor. This system goes beyond simply collecting and commenting on ideas, making the interaction a much more engrained part of the business processes.

From a relationship-building standpoint, Starbucks is valuing comments, collecting ideas, and continually putting them into action. By collaborating with and recognizing the customers who are helping make the organization better, Starbucks inherently understands the business value that social media can bring.

Enhancing Brand Awareness and Perception

To some degree, using any aspect of social media well inside an organization will inherently lead to better relationships and enhance the brand's perception. Social media can also allow an organization's brand to be repositioned or revived. A great example of this is BlendTec. Sure, they have always made a great blender, but as a product, they were not top of mind for the consumer. That is until they launched an ongoing series of videos called "Will It Blend?" This fun and quirky series, conducted by the organization's CEO Tom Dixon, attempts to use their blenders to destroy all sorts of products, from iPads (a personally painful episode) to pickled pigs' feet to light bulbs to a golf club (not a bad idea if you've seen us play golf). Tom will blend anything, and the audience loves the real connection with the organization.

The evidence that social media enhances a brand is not just supported by a few good examples. A 2009 Cone Consumer New Media Study showed 74 percent of consumers had a more positive impression of an organization after interacting with it using social media, and 64 percent had a more favorable impression of a brand if a friend interacted with the organization using social media.

TRAINING

Social media is one of those functions that just cannot be outsourced. An organization should not have a third party be its sole voice in social media and expect it to maintain its true authenticity. However, unless there is staff with proven experience in directing this function (which is generally not the case), training is something that can, and probably should, be initially conducted by a third party. While social media is more of an "organic" communications function, empowering staff that are not trained opens the door to multiple risks.

ORGANIZATIONAL STRUCTURES

There are a number of ways that the social media function can be integrated into an organization. Consulting firm Altimeter Group suggests the following approaches:

- **Organic**. The use of social media grows from several different sources in the organization. This approach generally occurs with larger organizations when communications are difficult to control. While the conversations appear authentic, the risk is providing an inconsistent customer experience, leading to potential reputational risk. While many social media initiatives start in this manner, it often leads to overall confusion and is very difficult to correct as the activities mature.
- **Centralized**. One business unit (generally corporate communications) manages all social aspects. This is best in highly regulated industries or organizations that are subjected to a great degree of scrutiny, but the risk that the social media function simply becomes another distribution point for press releases and traditional communications increases, thereby diminishing the likelihood for success.

- **Coordinated**. This structure is based on more of a committee system where one group assists other business units, teams, or locations in training and support. This group will also be primarily responsible for oversight and reporting to executive management. It is important that, to be successful, this group function as an enabler rather than hoarding information and primarily serving as a compliance unit.
- **Hub and spoke**. This is another model that is generally used by larger, global organizations, especially when there are cultural, governmental, or language differences. Groups are free to act as they see fit, yet still stay within a common customer experience. This is a costly model that, to be successful, requires executive support on a global basis and extensive cross-communication between all units.
- **Honeycomb**. This is generally more ideal than achievable, as it takes a unique corporate culture and a management team that embrace's social media as a core part of the business. This model enables everyone to actively participate in social media. It requires a cultural commitment and extensive training and support.

There is not necessarily a single best strategy or plan for an organization to use when it dives into the social media pool. Neither is there a single best way to integrate social media into that organization. The important point is to ensure that all aspects of the organization's approach to social media are aligned with the strategy, goals, and objectives of that organization's implementation plan.

CHAPTER 3

Monitoring and Measuring

At the heart of a successful social media program is a commitment to monitoring and measuring. As discussed previously, if you do nothing else in social media, listen to the conversations that are occurring about the organization, its stakeholders, the competition, and the industry; it will be one of the most significant ways to mitigate risk and provide insight. Remember, just because your organization decides not to engage in social media does not mean that people are not talking about you. Consumers are now more in control of the message and they will take to their social networks to talk about their feelings, opinions, and sentiments. And your organization and your brand will be in the crosshairs.

> "Consumers are in the midst of a conversation that isn't ours. The race is on to grow ears to learn what they are saying."
>
> —John Hayes, CMO, American Express

It is the aggregated sum of these conversations and the overall resulting sentiment that has a major impact on the organization's reputation management and brand equity. Traditional marketing and advertising are no longer the only drivers of how consumers view a brand and make purchasing decisions. They are looking for authentic opinions "from people like me" and are relying less on the traditional marketing messages. That is also why so many organizations have jumped into social media and, as discussed in the last chapter, many have done so without realizing that the business's objectives and its strategic social media plan have anything in common. That could not be further from the truth.

How It Can Go Wrong and What to Do

Without listening effectively, an organization faces the risk of either being disconnected from stakeholders (through a lack of participation) or, in the case of just jumping in and talking, alienating stakeholders by participating in the wrong venue, with irrelevant information, and in an inappropriate conversational style. In either case, the organization is exposed to a new level of risk that did not exist five (or even three) years ago.

Unfortunately, listening is not all it takes for success. It must be combined with learning, responding, measuring, and sharing. This is a key imperative for not only success, but also survival. Organizations that ignore social media will struggle to survive in this new communications era. Those that do not learn, respond, measure, and share will struggle to maintain their relevancy. However, those that take these components and make them part of a strategic approach to achieving business objectives will be better positioned to thrive. Because each component has its nuances, breaking each one down provides greater insight into how to identify a proper implementation and assist in assuring that risk is mitigated—all while adding value to the organization.

Listening

Not that long ago, organizations listened with customer comment cards, surveys, focus groups, and call monitoring. While this is still done today and can be effective in some areas, the true voice of the customers is occurring in their new natural habitat—social media. And they are not being asked to start the conversation. What was once limited to private conversations—face-to-face, on the phone, in writing—is now occurring digitally in posts, tweets, comments, podcasts, and videos. More important, this content is now publicly available and the organization has front row tickets to listen (and participate) in the conversation.

Further, in an age where everyone is (or can be) a publisher, the result is conversational scalability giving any one person or topic the ability to reach a massive number of people with a conversation that grows exponentially. For some, this is a tremendous opportunity to build awareness, increase donations, and turn fans into advocates for an organization or cause. However, when things go wrong, this scalability opens the door for a potentially manageable issue to reach a global audience. Seemingly innocent missteps can become major issues, and major issues can threaten the future of the organization.

If you think you are in control, you're fooling yourself. As soon as you start listening, you realize you're not in control. And letting go will yield more and better results.

—Charlene Li, author of *Groundswell*
and *Open Leadership* and founder
of Altimeter Group

Basic Listening

In social media, basic listening is a relatively easy process. It is a broad-based approach to monitoring conversations and covers the organization, its stakeholders, the competition, and the industry. While this broad-based approach may seem to lack focus, it is necessary to increase the likelihood of discovering new information. This approach is best used when just starting out with social media, as well as during the early discovery phases. Somewhat counterintuitively, it can also be used in situations where there are very limited resources.

Steps in Basic Listening

Step 1. Identify the keywords that surround your organization and brand. This should include corporate and brand names, stock symbols, and names of key staff (executive management and those that are highly visible to external stakeholders). In the same way, the list should include the names of competitors, their brand names, stock symbols, and key staff. The list should also include broad industry terms. As an example, a quick search using the free monitoring tool Social Mention (socialmention.com) revealed some of the obvious, and not so obvious, keywords that came up for the following brands (as of September 2010):
Starbucks: Coffee
JC Penney: Fashion, Mall
Raytheon: Defense, Exoskeleton
CitiGroup: Bank, CitiJobs
McDonald's: Nuggets, Health, Ronald
Deloitte: Consulting
JetBlue: Airways, Attendant, Steve Slater

By going through this exercise, a comprehensive list can be developed to capture the conversations.

This list should be monitored over time for relevancy, new issues that arise in the organization or industry, inclusion of new products, and any other changes that may seem appropriate.

Step 2. Identify the monitoring tools that will be used. In the appendices, there are a number of tools identified (some requiring payment, some free) that can aid in the listening efforts. While there is no one perfect solution, make sure that the list captures all the potential forms of content (blogs, microblogs, bookmarks, comments, events, images, news, video, audio, questions) as well as the major social networking platforms.

Step 3. Set up automated alerts that will notify the appropriate person or team when a keyword is mentioned. These alerts will generally be sent by e-mail. This is the data that will be used when it comes to learning.

These are the initial steps to begin listening to the conversation. It is by no means a comprehensive approach, but it is a start. What this gives the organization is a broad, general overview of the conversations that are occurring online. What it does not do is provide any indicator of the sentiment or influence this content has on the overall audience. Both sentiment and influence can be very important to measure, especially as the social media activities progress from listening to engaging.

It is also important to note that this is not a quick process that will transform an organization overnight. This is a commitment to understanding that the stakeholder is a publisher and has the ability to talk about an organization without its permission. It is a business imperative that cannot be ignored. This was well summarized by Anthony van der Hoek, director of Strategy and Business Solutions with the Coca-Cola Company, when he said, "It takes years, not weeks, to embed consumer conversations in an organization. Organizations need to address this now or it will be a huge challenge to catch up."

Advanced Listening

Advanced listening takes a slightly different direction and requires a more strategic approach involving more sophisticated tools that pinpoint opportunities to drive value. It takes place when the organization has taken greater steps in its social media implementation and has either put a formal strategy into place or has at least identified business objectives that can be impacted through the use of social media. It is important to note that basic listening should run concurrently with advanced listening; the difference being advanced listening seeks to identify specific areas of impact within the organization.

To identify the best areas for using advanced listening, the question "Where would a granular understanding of stakeholder behavior, sentiment, and influence have the greatest impact on the business?" must be answered. Examples might include customer service, recruitment, product innovations, and sales. The term *stakeholder* means much more than the traditional definition of *customer*. Other audiences such as current, past, and potential employees; vendors; analysts; members of the community; and potential business partners play a role in achieving business objectives.

Steps in Advanced Listening

Step 1. Determine the best opportunities to impact business objectives in the short term. This can include identifying areas of risk or unique issues that are occurring internally or externally that could have a near-term impact on the organization.

Step 2. Identify what you need to know to make an impact on the business objectives. While you will still need to identify the appropriate keywords, the focus will center more on the totality of the conversation, the context, and those in the conversation. For example, if the objective is to build a sustainable pipeline of potential professional-level staff, you would want to know who the current thought leaders are in the industry, who is engaged in the conversation, and how their thoughts are relevant to the type of people you are seeking. In this situation, you will most likely not find these people when searching for your brand; rather, you are more likely to find them with broader searches because they are publishing content that relates to the industry, their profession, or their particular skill set.

Step 3. Identify who will be in the conversation. This will determine the stakeholder involvement for each business objective. If the objective is to reduce customer issue resolution time, the people in the conversation will be customers that are outspoken in social networks about the organization and its products. By understanding who the stakeholder is, it is easier to identify the types of conversations that will occur.

Step 4. Determine where the most meaningful conversations are most likely to occur. Though you will be using a more sophisticated tool to listen to the conversations, some might be more meaningful than others. Understanding where your most valuable stakeholders congregate can create a subtle, but meaningful, difference in the insights you receive.

Step 5. Understand who in the organization is in the best position to gain actionable insights from the listening activities. If you are trying to understand what enhancements your customers feel your product could use to make it better, make sure the product manager and designers are part of the process. As we have mentioned

53

numerous times, to gain the most benefit and achieve objectives, social media cannot be a siloed activity. Make sure the right people are in the room.

Step 6. Determine which tools will be best able to help you listen and collect the right information. This becomes critical at this point in the process. There are a number of excellent tools and there is no one best solution available (a list is available in Appendix C, Common and Popular Social Media Monitoring Tools). Some are better suited than others and a detailed review should be conducted. The good thing is that most of them offer free trials, allowing the organization to put the tool to practical use before committing to one particular solution.

While the organization should always be listening at a basic level, advanced listening is where targeted data can produce actionable insights that help achieve business objectives while minimizing risks. However, data alone will not suffice; once the conversational data is collected, it is time to learn from that data to truly understand how to take the appropriate actions.

Learning

Here is a trap that many organizations fall into when getting started in social media. Too many organizations that are listening simply listen—and that's it. They might respond or submit an interesting post or comment, but the real value begins when true organizational learning results from listening.

Learning from social media insights can be either proactive or reactive, and both are not necessarily hard to accomplish. Reactive learning is done when content is published that directly or indirectly impacts the organization. For example, a comment might be posted about a competitor that sparks an idea that could be easily implemented in your organization. While the organization did not solicit this information, it still represents a great insight into potentially improving a customer's experience. The approach is similar to basic listening in that is it general and broad-based with insights coming from multiple sources.

Proactive learning comes from solicited feedback, requires engagement, and is aligned with the strategic plan and business objectives. With proactive learning, the organization is identifying key areas or issues that require greater feedback and insight. This learning is tied to a business objective with questions being posed to the appropriate target audience, in the right venue, and with the best conversational style. This approach is intended to prompt the best response from the stakeholder. For example, if an organization wants to drive additional revenue through special "one-day deals," posts could be made to the fans and followers on Facebook and Twitter to determine if these are the best venues. The organization might also send customers an e-mail. This is all meant to test and measure the differences among e-mail, Facebook, and Twitter to determine which channel will drive the best response. (Even in a proactive learning situation, reactive learning and traditional competitive intelligence should also be included to measure what other similar organizations are doing to create a meaningful differentiator in the marketplace.)

Another aspect of learning related to social media is that it should not reside in its own silo and exclude other forms of learning. Ideally, the organization should be in a continuous learning and improvement mode, with social media simply being one aspect of the overall process.

Responding

While organizations can listen, and some will learn from their listening, it is the act of responding that separates the winners from the crowd of wannabes. Dell, rising from a major customer service issue in 2005, made listening, learning, and responding (in a social media environment) a priority, enabling the company to implement more than 425 customer-generated ideas as of mid-2010.

One key to putting these insights into action is ensuring that the right people are included in the process; people who understand the nature of the situation. This is yet another reason why social media should not be siloed within the organization. (Seems we may have said this before, but it can't be said enough.) Great insights can be developed, but if the "social media guy" approaches product engineers with a new idea without the context or meaning to support it, innovation can be stifled and dismissed. Successful programs have a team approach that values and understands the voice of the stakeholder and respects the way the insight was developed and conveyed.

> Social media is the best way to reach your most influential customers, and the only way to reach your most cynical ones.
>
> —Michael Troiano, Principal, Holland-Mark

Measuring

The next component of successful monitoring is measuring, and this is where it can get more complicated. Determining the measurements that truly evaluate how social media is helping the organization meet its business objectives is where real value is created. In too many cases, the metrics being collected and reported on are not metrics; they are simply activities that have no real intrinsic value. Figures such as the number of fans, followers, and page views are not drivers of the business unless these interactions actually help the organization meet its objectives.

Even if quality metrics are identified, simply collecting the data without learning or responding (either internally or to the stakeholder) and without reporting on the data collected is, for the most part, a waste of resources. This is also one of the leading reasons executives struggle with social media—it simply isn't helping solve the issues that are on the top of their minds. Fans, followers, and page views cannot be directly attributed to hiring and retaining the best talent, improving product development, increasing customer satisfaction, or driving sales. They are simply nice metrics—meaningless, but nice.

For social media to be of value to the organization, it must be held accountable for business objectives. If not aligned with business objectives, the social media program has a greater likelihood of failure and exposing the organization to reputational risk. A side benefit is that, by holding these programs accountable, they are far more likely to be allocated proper resources, staffing, and training.

Common Metrics

Metrics will vary for each organization and functional area that is using social media. Below are a few of the more common measurements grouped by types of business objectives.

Brand Recognition and Awareness

- **Stakeholder engagement**. Includes number of comments, bookmarks, images, pictures, and videos that mention the organization in some fashion.
- **Advocate engagement**. Includes the people (nonstaff) who are more actively promoting your organization. Metrics within this category include:
  - Number of advocates.
  - Advocate frequency. How often they are mentioning your organization.

- Advocate influence and reach. How influential these people are compared to the overall stakeholders and how many people they reach.
- Advocate impact. The level of impact these people have; enhancing the sentiment, increasing the number of advocates, and so on.

- **Share of voice**. The number of mentions your organization has compared to the total number of mentions for your organization plus its competitors.
- **Sentiment**. The overall sentiment from the conversations that are occurring about the organization. A deeper dive into this can reveal the net sentiment. This can also include a comparison of sentiment for your organization to its competitors.

Customer Service

- **Issue submission percentage**. The percentage of issues submitted using social media channels compared to total number of issues from all channels.
- **Issue resolution rate**. The number of issues that are successfully resolved using social media.
- **Issue resolution time**. The time it takes to resolve a customer service issue through social media versus other communications channels. These results should also be compared to the overall goals for all channels.
- **Customer satisfaction rate**. The satisfaction level of customers who resolved issues through social media channels. This should also be compared to the overall goal as well as the results for other channels.
- **External customer engagement**. How much customers are discussing the service level provided through their social networks. This should be measured related to sentiment, influence, and reach to gauge the net impact.

- **Financial impact**. The financial impact in terms of expenses (and revenue, if applicable) from using social media as a customer service channel.

Human Resources

- **Potential candidate engagement**. The number of potential candidates that have engaged with the organization and its staff.
- **New hire rate**. The number of candidates that were hired using social media as a recruiting tool. This should also be compared to the overall goal and to the results of other channels.
- **Employee retention rate**. The retention rate for employees that have been hired from social media sources compared to other hiring sources.
- **Employee sentiment**. The overall sentiment of current and past employees. These measures should also include influence and reach to gauge the net impact.
- **Financial impact**. The financial impact in terms of expenses from using social media as a recruiting channel.
- **Employee influence, reach, and impact**. For organizations that embrace the use of social media for its employees, determine the overall influence, reach, and impact they have on stakeholders, competitors, and the industry. The goal here is to have employees emerge as well-regarded thought leaders.

Innovation

- **Issues reported and number of conversations**. The number of issues reported, the number that led to discussions, and the number upon which the organization acted.
- **Ideas submitted**. The total number of ideas submitted by stakeholders that can help improve the organization, its products, or its services.

- **Idea and issue impact**. Of the total number of ideas and issues reported or discovered; the overall impact in terms of satisfaction; purchase or retention rates cost savings (or increases); and the like.

Sales and Marketing

- **Leads generated and converted**. The number of prospective customers that originated from social media activities and the number converted into paying customers or clients. Additionally, the cost of acquiring these customers compared to other channels.
- **Revenue**. The gross and net revenue as a result of social media activities, including comparing this against budgets and goals. This should include determining the percentage of total revenue. For nonprofits, this can include fundraising and contributions.
- **New customer acquisition**. The number of new customers that were added as a result of the social media activities.
- **Customer retention and repeat purchase rate**. The retention rate and repeat purchase rate (including revenues) for customers that were acquired from or are using social media as a sales channel. This includes a comparison against other channels.
- **Average purchase amount**. The average purchase amount of these purchases compared to other channels.
- **Customer lifetime value**. The lifetime value of customers that use social media compared to other channels.

Sharing

The final component of successful monitoring is sharing—everything. One of the keys to preventing social media activities from climbing into a silo is sharing conversations, ideas, suggestions, responses, impact, and metrics. The more that information (including successes and lessons learned) is shared throughout the organization, the greater the likelihood that (1) social media will be applied to drive even greater value in more areas of the organization; (2) social media will be embraced as more than a compliance issue; (3) the voice of the customer will be respected and add value to the organization in new ways; (4) social media will be embraced by executive management as a strategic method of driving organizational value; and (5) risks related to the use of social media will be reduced.

CHAPTER 4

Social Media Policies

In the same 2009 national research study cited in Chapter 2, Russell Herder and Ethos Business Law found that 69 percent of the organizations that they had surveyed did not have a social media policy in place and only 10 percent have conducted relevant training. The study also reported that 40 percent of organizations have blocked access to social networking sites and prohibit their use. In today's mobile-enabled world, it is somewhat naive for an organization to believe it can actually block the use of social media within its four walls. While it might appear that blocking access would be the safe route to protecting the organization, employees will simply find ways around the ban (either through mobile devices or participating outside the workplace), potentially creating even greater issues in the long term. To truly help mitigate the risks of social media, organizations should define not only a policy but a strategic approach to employee engagement, making this emerging communications medium part of the culture.

What is also surprising is the enormous disconnect between how an employer and employee view social media usage. While both agree that social media can be a risk, the

2009 Deloitte LLP's *Ethics and Workplace* Survey indicated that 74 percent of working Americans believe it is easy to damage a brand's reputation via sites such as Facebook, Twitter, and YouTube, though relatively few organizations are actively creating strategies and policies. Also interesting from this survey is that 53 percent of employees believe that their social networking activity is none of the employers' business; 49 percent indicate that, even if there were a policy in place, it would not affect their behavior; and one-third stated they never consider what their boss, colleagues, or clients think before posting materials online. On the employer side, 60 percent of executives state the organization has a "right to know" how employees portray themselves and their organizations online, with 30 percent acknowledging informal monitoring practices.

So perhaps it's no wonder that so many organizations have failed to implement a policy. If social media usage can't be blocked and if employees don't care if there is a policy in place to govern the practice, what is an organization to do? The answer is to develop a policy *and* a training program for all employees that acknowledges social media, understands it has become a significant part of how the majority of people interact today, sets boundaries, and embraces it as a part of the organizational culture.

Unfortunately there is no generally accepted template for creating a social media policy. Some of the best are a single page while others are 20 pages or more. However, the vast majority (and most successful) are written in plain language and embrace the appropriate conversational style that fits with social media itself. If the organization does not feel completely comfortable with developing, implementing, and training staff on the policy, it should consider retaining a consultant that understands the nuances and can not only include best practices, but also integrate them into the organization's culture.

The Social Media Policy Team

The first thing to consider when developing the policy is who should be part of the team in charge of its development. While perhaps not intimately involved in the development, executive management should be part of the process and fully buy in to the spirit and intent of the policy and training. Having these senior leaders (and the board of directors) play an active part in this policy is a proactive step to help gain support of the policy and mitigate potential risks.

The core team should consist of members of the marketing, public relations, human resources, IT, product development, internal audit, and legal teams, as well as any dedicated or occasional social media practitioners that are actively engaging in social media on the organization's behalf. This could include customer service, subject matter experts, product managers, and others. This core team should also understand that, because the social media space continues to evolve rapidly, the social media policy must be considered a living document that is revisited at least semiannually to ensure relevance.

Internal and External Stakeholders

To ensure a comprehensive view of the social media landscape within an organization, both internal and external stakeholders must be considered. From an internal perspective, the policy will set guidelines for what employees can and cannot do, as well as what the organization will and will not do. For the external stakeholders, the focus is on what the public can and cannot say on the organization's online sites and what the organization will and will not do to monitor and curate these interactions. This gives the organization the ability to reject or delete content on its site that does not meet the requirements of the policy for external stakeholders.

Elements of an Effective Social Media Policy for Internal Stakeholders

Overall Position on Social Media

The policy should provide employees with guidance on the organization's approach to social media. For some, like Zappos.com, it is embedded as a core part of the organization's culture. For others, it is quite restrictive with very limited acceptance. By communicating the organization's position, it is easier for employees to understand not only what the guidelines are but the rationale for why there were developed.

Rules Still Apply

While it is great to talk about empowerment and embracing social media, it is also important to clearly convey that there are rules that apply. This includes being very clear that employees (in their professional and personal usage) do not have a right to privacy with respect to social networking. It is also important to state that the organization has the right to monitor employee use of social media without regard to location. While this might not change behavior or even how an employee feels about the policy, it is included to protect the organization. It must be clearly stated and include the consequences if the policy is not followed.

Many organizations might discover there are several overlapping issues that involve existing policies and procedures from other areas within the organization. These might include:

- IT controls for compliance with username and password policies

- Employee confidentiality, especially compliance with sexual harassment, discrimination, defamation, and the Health Insurance Portability and Accountability Act (HIPAA) laws
- Employee usage of the Internet for nonwork activities
- Confidentiality and disclosure of the organization's intellectual property

While these policies most likely exist in the organization, it is important to reiterate that these same policies also apply to the use of social media.

Establishing Boundaries

Accepting that the organization cannot (1) control the message and (2) actually block the use of social media by its employees, an effective social media policy will be based on trust, empowering employees to engage and do the right thing—within boundaries. While it will differ for each organization, it is essential to:

- Clearly communicate what the employees can and cannot do on social networks.
- State what the organization will and will not do—this not only includes the monitoring practices for employees (both listening to conversations and monitoring activity from an IT perspective), but can also include what social media tools will and will not be used by the organization.
- Include other policies that might be affected by social media (including ethics, confidentiality, harassment, etc.).
- Provide guidance on what the public can and cannot say or do on the organization's online properties.

Communications Considerations

To help engender employee trust and acceptance, it is important that the policy not only affirm that the communications style should be individualized and authentic, but that there are considerations that need to be addressed before engaging with any audience.

- **Add value.** It should be stressed that the majority of communications by an internal stakeholder should be designed to add value to the relevant audience they are engaging. Communications that do not add value become noise and the conversation becomes less interesting. Posts that simply state "Happy Tuesday! It's a beautiful day here at XVZ Corp" are fine if done occasionally, but should not represent a significant portion of the conversation.
- **Conversational style and authenticity.** It is also important to include language that stresses the need for individuals to converse with the proper conversational style and authenticity. In other words, be yourself. Failure to include this could result in content and conversations that are too formal with corporate jargon.
- **Honesty and respect.** Include reaffirming to internal stakeholders that when they engage in online conversations, they must always do so with honesty and respect for the other person—especially if they are discussing competitors. The key here is to include language that the employees should do no harm to anyone involved in the conversation and that they are to respond to ideas without engaging in personal attacks.
- **Transparency and disclosure.** The policy must include language that, when an employee is discussing the organization, industry, stakeholders, or competition, they must fully disclose and be transparent about the relationship between themselves and the organization. Not only is this an ethical issue, but also one that can have legal implications with government agencies such as the Federal Trade Commission (FTC). A link to the FTC Guidelines on Disclosure is contained in Appendix A, Chapter Links.

- **Confidentiality**. This is another key element of the policy and, because it is probably already included in other organizational policies, should mirror those other policies. As employees begin to use social media more freely, there is an increased risk that they may share proprietary or confidential information. That is why it is important for the policy to provide specific emphasis on areas related to dealing with intellectual property, security, financial reporting, press releases, and human resource issues.
- **Ownership and registering properties**. Communicate to employees what content is owned by the employee and what is owned by the organization. If an employee maintains a blog on the industry and is considered to be a subject matter expert, and this blog is hosted and supported by the organization, who owns that content? The answers may not be clear-cut, so the policy needs to include these guidelines. In certain cases, individual agreements might be necessary. There are also instances where the organization requires employees who create social media content about the industry to register that content with the social media team (for monitoring purposes).
- **Endorsements and recommendations**. This is another interesting issue that needs to be addressed in a comprehensive policy. In most organizations, it is the policy for the human resource team to decline any recommendation or endorsement relating to a former employee. However, that policy is often not shared beyond the internal human resources team. This can result in an employee, particularly supervisors of former employees, providing recommendations and endorsements on sites such as LinkedIn.com. The takeaway here is, if the employee was terminated for cause and the employee's supervisor posts a favorable recommendation, there could be increased risk to the organization if the terminated employee brings legal action.

- **Degree of personal and professional use**. This will vary considerably depending on the organization, but with guidelines that are built on trust and personal responsibility, it is often advisable to not set boundaries that are too restrictive. Many successful policies address the level of professionalism and productivity required by the employee to effectively complete the work required.

Conflicts of Interests

There are instances when conflicts of interest may arise. This could occur in the case of a pending merger, acquisition, significant business transaction, or legal issue that directly or indirectly involves the organization. The social media policy should provide guidance to the employee on how to deal with these issues, what they can and cannot discuss, and how to elevate issues or situations when the situation is unclear.

Responding to Comments

This might seem easy, but it has a few twists that need to be included in a comprehensive policy. The organization should have a position on what it will and will not respond to on any social media property. This should be aligned with honesty and respect as well as transparency and disclosure. It is also important that everyone understand that just because something is posted online about the organization or a stakeholder it does not always require a response. Beyond matters of confidentiality and some of the other points discussed above, there are, quite simply, those who want to start an online conflict or will misstate the truth to advance a cause. There are no absolute guidelines here, but a good policy will address these issues and provide employees with guidance on how to address them, as well as an escalation process should a conversation go awry.

Follow the Law

There are several laws and regulations—in the United States, Europe, and throughout the world—that are designed to govern social media conversations. Some of these specifically address communications in social media, while others, such as the U.S. Securities and Exchange Commission (SEC) and the FTC, have regulations on the dissemination of information (timing and content). It is important that the legal team, as well as functional teams that are well versed in these regulations, include guidance on how to be in compliance.

Consequences

Effectively developing accountability and consequences for an employee's actions (either deliberate or accidental) is vital to the policy. When more than 50 percent of employees don't care or won't change their social networking behavior, it is most likely because (1) there is not a policy in place with the proper training, and (2) there are no consequences for inappropriate behavior. Consequences should be in alignment with other such policies within the organization, as well as those embedded within its culture. Some organizations are very trusting and open; whereas others have decided (or are required) to be more conservative and closed. Whatever the case, consequences should be fair and reasonable.

Crisis Communications

It is important to include language that clearly states that employees cannot represent themselves to the media (or anyone else) as a spokesperson for that organization without expressed permission. It is also worth noting that, according to the Russell Herder Ethos Business Law survey, 87 percent of organizations do not address social media as part of the crisis communications plan. Appendices A and D include U.S. Air Force Web sites for information on the triage and response to crisis communications issues as related to social media.

Elements of an Effective Social Media Policy for External Stakeholders

It is fair to assume that, if an organization maintains a presence on social networks, these should be actively moderated and curated. When an organization is actively engaging across a number of networks (including its own), there will be occasions when conversations will have to be deleted or rejected. This is something that should be done with great care to quell concerns about favoritism or overcontrol of the conversation. For example, consider the impact on the organization's reputation if favorable comments on an organization's products are allowed but any negative comments are deleted. That is clearly not in the spirit of transparency and authenticity. A similar such issue can arise when negative comments are deleted for an advertiser or sponsor of the organization but are maintained for nonadvertisers.

The policy for site moderation should be fair and clear for both internal and external audiences. While the organization is not obligated to share its internal policy with external stakeholders, the external policy should be prominently posted and made available to all stakeholders. The external policy should be included in the training for internal stakeholders. The next sections discuss elements for consideration and inclusion.

Commenting Allowed or Disallowed While commenting on posts should generally be allowed to foster engagement and conversation, there are some instances when commenting is inappropriate. Some content may be for the straight dissemination of news and information and the organization may not feel it is appropriate to engage in a conversation in this venue. While this is on a case-by-case basis, including the rationale for allowing or disallowing comments can be effective guidance to external stakeholders.

Comment Moderation   This details why the organization might (or will) delete or reject content placed on a social media site maintained by the organization:

- **Offensive language**. This should simply not be tolerated and content should be deleted or rejected.
- **Attacks and threats**. Whether they are personal or directed to the organization, this is not professional and comments should be deleted or rejected.
- **Off topic**. Social media sites present great opportunities for people to post ads, links to off-topic sites, and so on. If the content is not on topic or not valuable to the audience, it is fair to delete or reject the post.
- **Proprietary information**. It doesn't matter if confidential information is about your organization or a competitor, anything considered "proprietary" should be removed immediately to forestall any potential legal issues.
- **Banning**. The organization's policy on banning a person for commenting or accessing these sites is part of the rules of engagement and should be included.

Proactive and Reactive Management   It can be helpful to external stakeholders to know whether the organization is proactively or reactively managing and curating its social media sites. Proactive management will generally approve a post before it goes live. This involves reviewing the content using the commenting guidelines and within a specified period of time. Reactive management generally allows all posts to go live immediately with a reactive monitoring for management. Either situation has its pros and cons and will vary by organization. However, providing the guidance to the stakeholder allows for a common understanding of the rules of engagement.

Social Media Account Disclosure This is another element that can be helpful to external stakeholders and demonstrates transparency and disclosure. In this section, the organization discloses the sites that it maintains. This is helpful to identify what is and is not an organization property. This especially helps the external stakeholder avoid issues with phishing or engaging with people who falsely portray them to be representatives. This should also disclose the account names by which organizational representatives can be identified. (See the previous discussion about @StefanieatDell in Chapter 3.) Letting users know who the representatives are and how they can be identified helps provide external stakeholders with a greater degree of confidence in their online communications.

SERVICE-LEVEL AGREEMENTS Another key to setting the proper expectations is to develop and disclose appropriate service-level agreements (SLAs) with external stakeholders on a number of different issues. Some of the more popular include:

- **Hours of operation and response time.** Not all organizations can staff 24/7 or even consistently during a workday. Stating any formal (or informal) hours of operation and the issue response time can help set the proper expectations with external stakeholders.
- **Error correction.** Provide information on how the organization will address error correction and the expected response time for correcting a legitimate error.

■ **How the organization will disclose and comment**. It is appropriate to provide guidance as to what type of information the organization will disclose, how it will be disclosed, and how it will comment on various issues. It is fair to assume that not all conversations are best suited for social networks, and it is also fair for the organization to disclose what it will be and will not be willing to disclose and comment on in these networks.

The other important aspects to consider in managing SLAs is developing appropriate metrics around each SLA and continually monitoring performance to assure that external stakeholders' expectations are being met properly.

Social Media Policy Training

If there is an area in social media policy development that has the greatest place for improvement, it is in the training. It is great to go through all the work of appointing a cross-functional team, writing the strategies and policies, and developing metrics. However, if it is not effectively communicated with the proper training, how are employees supposed to understand what it means to them?

Training on social media (not just the policy) should be ongoing and inclusive of everyone. The strategy, philosophy, and policies should be open and transparent, allowing everyone to understand how the organization will engage with its internal and external stakeholders. If there is not a skilled internal staff member with experience in social media and training in general, it might be appropriate to look to an external consultant.

Besides the overall review of the social media strategy and plan, a detailed review of the policy should be conducted with continuing education at least annually for those not directly involved and semiannually for those directly involved. This should include specifics on each aspect of the policy as well as consequences. Again, there are numerous external programs and courses (online and onsite) conducted by the Word of Mouth Marketing Association (WOMMA) as well as other trade groups and private consultants and firms.

Here are a few elements that should be included in a social media training program:

- **Concept of community.** It is important to stress that engagement on behalf of the organization means that person is part of the community and, much like any real-world community, has an implied duty to be a good citizen and serve and grow that community responsibly.
- **Consider the members of the community.** This aligns with using the conversational style, adding value, and being authentic. To really grow any community, it is important that the person is as engaging and helpful to another person online as they are within their own community with their neighbors and friends. The content might be different, but the spirit of helping and serving is the same.
- **Transparency, disclosure, and confidentiality.** Not only is this ethically correct, but in many cases there are regulations and guidelines that have a legal impact. It is also important to train staff on what can and cannot be said, as well as the difference between personal and organization-owned accounts and properties.
- **Copyright and attribution.** While the tone might be more relaxed, it does not mean that plagiarism and copyright infringement are discounted.

It is also important that these training materials be developed in plain language with an understanding that many may not feel comfortable or be familiar with social media tools. With this in mind, a series of training classes on "what is social media," "social media tools and how to use them," and other programs can help staff decide to engage or not—and if they do engage, how to do it correctly. Social media training should also include employee testing and internal certification before being allowed to represent the organization on social networks.

CHAPTER 5

Social Media Risks

The greatest risk related to social media is what organizations *do not know*. This includes not only what they do not know about social media but also the conversation that is going on without them and what is happening to their brand in the process. As noted in Chapter 1, while 58 percent of corporate executives agree there should be discussions related to the reputational risks from social networking, only 15 percent are actively addressing them. It would appear that this reluctance to address these risks arises from one aspect—the pervasiveness of social media is moving so fast that organizations have not had time to understand there are risks and, maybe more important, they do not feel qualified to understand the risks.

However, while aspects of social media are cloaked in the special terminology that arises with any new paradigm shift, the basic risks faced by any organization related to social media are not appreciably different than those they are used to facing. It is just the unique nature of social media that makes these risks take on new shapes and forms. To better understand the applicable risks, it is easiest to look at them within the two primary building blocks of any organization: strategy/planning and execution/process.

Strategy and Planning Risks

As with any operation within an organization, the chances of it succeeding in its social media activities is greatly diminished without a basic understanding of its strategy and a set of plans developed around those strategies. Chapter 2 provided a lot of detail related to social media strategies and planning. You will see that reflected in the following information related to social media risks that require particular attention.

Lack of Strategy

As previously noted, the success of any endeavor is highly dependent on the establishment of a solid strategy. (Even no strategy is actually a strategy.) In most situations, a risk assessment takes for granted the existence of a strategy; moving directly to the adequacy of that strategy and how it aligns to operations. However, because of the fast-moving applications of social media in the world (and because so many executives do not have a good understanding of its use and impact on business), many organizations have not even undertaken an analysis to determine whether a strategy is necessary.

Social media, at its very basic, is a communication tool. As such, it should be addressed as would be any other communication channel. The organization must develop strategies around how social media will (or will not) be used. Toward that end, three issues are considered next in evaluating the risks related to the lack of a strategy: (1) ignoring social media, (2) equating nonparticipation with noninvolvement, and (3) participating without an articulated strategy.

Ignoring Social Media

Ignoring social media is not the same thing as making the decision to not be involved in social media. Rather, this is the risk that the organization, without any understanding or analysis of the strategic ramifications, ignores what is going on in social media. Organization executives may have seen some blogs and remember hearing about MySpace or AOL, but they have dismissed it all as the antics of the narcissistic hoi polloi. As an example, the CEO may make the unilateral decision that even researching social media would be a waste of time and money. In other words, the decision is made without exploring the advancements, opportunities, and ramifications of social media on the business.

Again, this is not related to an informed decision to not be involved. Executives who study the social media situation, analyze the organization's role in social media, and determine that it does not fit the organization's profile, strategy, or goals, are not exposing the organization to this specific risk. Such are the makings of every real strategic decision. (If you are concerned about the specific decision, then you are looking at a different set of risks.) Ultimately, this risk relates to the organization not understanding the potential impacts of social media and therefore making no actual decision.

> Social media is the same today as it was yesterday. It's just now reached a critical mass; it's just too hard to ignore. You don't want to be "that guy" or "that brand" who refuses to adapt to change and loses touch with reality.
>
> —Julia Roy, Senior Manager, New Media, Coach, Inc.

Equating Nonparticipation with Noninvolvement

The next risk relates to those organizations that have made an informed decision to not be involved in social media. That decision, with proper deliberation and discussion (as noted previously), is not a problem in itself. However, some organizations feel that because they will not be participating in social media, they do not need to be worried about the communications and conversations that are occurring. If only one message comes out clearly from this book, it should be that your organization is involved whether it wants to be or not.

As we have noted, a conversation is going on about your organization. "They" are talking about your products and services, your customers and employees, and, most important, your brand. Accordingly, any organization that takes no action to monitor those conversations—to at least be active in listening—is exposing itself to customer service, brand, human resources, and reputational risks that might arise in locations where they decided not to look. This is the risk that the organization, although it has decided not to actively participate in the social media frenzy, has wrongly determined it does not need to establish an appropriate social media monitoring process.

Participating without an Articulated Strategy

Many organizations have made the calculated move to jump into social media. However, far too often those calculations have led to them jumping in without any idea why, how, or where to jump, and what to do once they have jumped there. It's a basic of business—make your decisions based on the overall strategy of the organization. However, because social media is new and many people do not understand the full ramifications, organizations throw a couple of people at the project (often those "new interns who seem to understand that Internet stuff") in hopes that something good will happen.

It is interesting to note that many of the strategies related to social media parallel the strategies organizations already establish over advertising and communications. Organizations spend vast resources (time, money, people) ensuring these are handled appropriately. Yet a part-timer may be set the task to "build us an Internet presence."

There are many different aspects of articulating a strategy and, for an organization to successfully dive into the social media pool, they must take all these into account. However, there are some points about coordinating this strategy that are particularly pertinent.

First, has an overall direction been established for all (and let us repeat, all) aspects of social media? An important risk is that there might be disparate strategies for the different media channels. And this may be different than the direction that is given to employees who are participating on other professional blogs. If the conversation from one side of the mouth does not match that from the other, your customers may be confused, distracted, and, maybe worse, turned off by the organization's different messages. While there might be different messages for various stakeholder audiences, there must be a strong alignment between all the messages sent (through social media or any other form of communication) to maintain the brand's integrity.

Second, does the overall direction for social media parallel the direction proscribed for other aspects of the organization's image—areas such as corporate responsibility, advertising, and public relations? Just as there are issues with potential disconnects among the various social media, similar disconnects between social media messaging and all other corporate communications will only cause consternation with the customers. It is important to point out that the conversational style might be different from formal corporate messaging, but there should be a consistency with the end result of all messaging.

Third (and maybe most important), has the organization even identified what image it wants to project in social media? Organizations should determine whether their current image matches what they are trying to achieve with social media and make the appropriate changes. This does not mean demolishing the existing image, but it can mean putting a new spin on the existing image. For example, it is not necessary (nor is it probably a good idea) to use identical advertising strategies, but the changes in approach for social media would not necessarily mean redoing the organization's overall advertising strategy. At the end of the day, all aspects of communication should be telling the same story or, at the very least, telling stories that mesh.

Strategy Is Inadequate

Chapter 2 provided background on what should be considered when developing a social media strategy. The same elements should be considered when determining whether the strategy that has been established is adequate. In broad terms, the following risks should be considered:

- Is the strategy real or simply a tactical use of social media tools?
- Is there a clear alignment between the social media activities and the organization's business objectives?
- Do these activities represent a long-term commitment or a series of strategic experiments?
- Is the social media strategy incorporated into the other existing strategic plans?
- Have the target audiences been identified that will help achieve the business objectives?
- Have the proper social media channels and conversational style been identified to best engage the target audiences?
- Have the social media activities received adequate resources in terms of staffing and funding?

Strategy, but No Plan

The next important issue related to social media strategy is actual development of a plan. For social media, this important document is the link between the executives' beautiful plan of a utopian Internet presence and the individual steps being taken on a daily basis to make sure it is accomplished.

As has been mentioned many times, social media is moving quickly; so quickly that organizations find themselves moving forward on several different fronts. This results in people within the organization moving forward on the actual implementation of ideas that are not fully formed. And, in this case, it behooves those who are developing the strategy to move quickly so everyone understands where they are going.

In their hurry, people think that a strategy is the actual plan and they start moving forward. Below, we talk about the aspects of planning that are important to a social media environment. However, the ultimate point is that, as with any other operation, strategy leads to plans, which lead to execution. The quick movement of social media means that any one of these steps can be omitted (including, surprisingly, execution), and the importance of risks related to missing links in that chain is much higher.

Lack of a Governance Structure

We talk about governance in some detail in Chapter 6, but there are some risk considerations that are worth bringing up at this point.

No Single Group Proving Oversight   It is not unusual for separate departments in larger organizations to take completely different tacks on social media. Very often, a single department will have a champion for social media—someone who has seen what it can do and convinces the department head to move forward. At the same time, another department has decided it is unnecessary to be involved. Two departments have now established separate strategies within the same organization. Six months later, a third department (unaware of what the first has done) has its own champion and they go off and start their own presence. There is no communication, no standardized approach, and no awareness at the top that the customers may be getting mixed messages.

It should be apparent from this description, as well as our previous discussions on risk, that there must be an alignment of message, brand, and image. To best achieve this, oversight of all social media projects should be centered with one executive, board, task force, committee, or similar group. This group or person will ensure that all actions are in accordance with the overall desires of executive management, communications remain on message, and the overall objectives of the social media strategy are being met.

No Guidelines for Elevating Issues Once a person or group is charged with oversight, it is important to establish how much information that individual or group needs to have available. As with any operation, they cannot be tied too closely to the day-to-day operations, but it must be clear when they need to be brought into the loop—whether during planned meetings or on a situational basis. Similarly, it should be clear when that person or group needs to elevate issues to the president, board, CEO, and so forth.

With social media, an important aspect of elevating issues is ensuring that the group to whom information is provided fully understands the background and ramifications of the issues. With most other aspects of business, issues are elevated to people who have extensive backgrounds in the business or industry. But the issues with social media change quickly, and today's nonissue may be tomorrow's nuclear explosion.

No Involvement from Assurance Partners We explain this in more detail in the discussion of governance in Chapter 6. However, the point of a governance process is to ensure that everyone who might understand the risks and related responses is involved in the development and oversight of objectives, policies, and processes established for the organization's use of social media. Accordingly, the failure to include the departments responsible for such areas as risk and compliance can result in deadly oversights.

New Social Media Opportunities Are Missed

Trying to keep up with the changes going on with social media can be futile. It seems that every few days something new comes out, then dies just as quickly. However, it also seems that about the time you dismiss one of those crazy ideas, it becomes the cornerstone of change. (Come on, how many of us really thought that limiting our thoughts to 140 characters or less would be a model for current communication?)

No one can be expected to guess what the next big thing will be. However, organizations must be aware of what is going on to ensure they do not miss out on the growing opportunities. A process should be established to monitor changes in social media with the intent of identifying ones that will be of value to the organization. In particular, the organization should look for changes that are being adopted by everyone (meaning the organization should be a part of that group), or changes that represent a niche area that will be invaluable to the organization because of its business, profession, distribution method, and so on. This does not mean jumping on everything—that is a faster route to failure than waiting too long. There is a balancing act between being too fast and too slow—and organizations must monitor the latest developments.

Not Considering Regulatory Requirements

Most organizations recognize the need to consider regulatory risks in their operations, in many instances establishing separate departments responsible for ensuring such compliance. However, there are some different aspects that relate to social media. One of the more important is that organizations may not be recognizing the different aspects that existing laws and regulations take with the advent of social media. For example, in some industries, there are specific regulations related to communication between the organization and its customers. In particular, there are various regulations (depending on the industry) related to how quickly the organization must respond to customer complaints. Almost all interpretations now consider any such posting to an organization's social media as triggering these requirements. Similarly, regulatory bodies have also determined that any social media communications coming from the organization or its representatives fall under their requirements. That simple tweet may now be regulated.

At the same time, federal and state agencies are developing new laws specific to the social media environment. Accordingly, organizations must expand their reviews related to changes in laws and regulations to include all social media issues.

Lack of a Social Networking Policy

No matter what the organization's decision regarding its participation in social media, there is a need for an organizationwide policy for all employees relating to the use of social media. A social networking policy lays out, for all employees, the organization's guidelines, rules, and regulations regarding employee conduct on social media. Even if the policy is that employees should never do anything, it must still be articulated.

Many of the risks that we have discussed should be addressed in this policy. But as much as possible, the policy should include very specific information on what can be done, what sites are allowed, and the organization's overall policies on social media.

What you want in your social networking policy is obviously dependent on the type of organization with which you are involved. However, as a recap from Chapter 4, the following areas should be included:

- The overall objective of the social networking policy and the organization's approach to social media.
- The pertinent rules that apply to the use of social media throughout the organization.
- The social media boundaries and communications considerations:
  - Who is responsible for postings to the organization's social media—department, titles, and names, if applicable.
  - The employee's role in the organization's social media conversation.
  - The employee's responsibilities and limitations outside their employee/employer relationship.
  - The need for transparency, disclosure, and how to address any conflicts of interest.
  - A description of how to ensure compliance with applicable laws.
- A description of taboo areas and Web sites that may be blocked.
- A statement on proprietary and confidential materials (including sensitive information about the organization, its customers, and its employees).
- Where to turn in the event problems are identified (especially those that could result in a crisis communications situation).
- Where to turn if employees find they are having problems.
- A connection with the organization's code of conduct and ethics guidelines.
- Guidelines related to all types of media (video, music, etc.), not just the written word.

Execution and Process Risks

As every auditor knows, the organization that addresses strategic risks has fought only half the battle. Strategy is nothing without execution, and the mitigation of strategic risk is nothing without addressing the risks to execution and operations. As with our discussions related to strategic risks, there are many execution risks that are the same whether you are looking at social media or any other aspect of the organization. What follows is an analysis of the risks that take on different aspects because of the unique nature of social media.

Lack of or Valueless Metrics

Just like any other project, process, or initiative, appropriate metrics must be established to ensure the organization's social media initiatives are achieving what the organization hopes to accomplish. So the first risk is that no metrics have been established. As has been mentioned with many other aspects of social media, the area has grown so fast that such measures are often overlooked. Keep in mind, inappropriate metrics can be even more detrimental than a lack of metrics as this provides a false sense of security that something is being measured and monitored.

Chapter 3 laid out some of the many measurements for success that can exist for social media. One thing that becomes quickly apparent is that there are many more ways to measure the performance of social media than anyone would want to measure. The selection of metrics has to align the social media activity with the overall business objectives of the organization. For example, assume that the organization is measuring the number of Twitter followers. If Twitter followers are meant to drive sales, then more detailed metrics focusing on Twitter's success as a sales channel would be appropriate. As with most social media platforms, the raw number of friends, followers, or fans is a useless metric without context. It is necessary to determine the degree to which these people are engaged with the brand by actively publishing content, commenting, replying, and re-tweeting messages. Furthermore, what is the overall sentiment of the conversations? Just because there is an increase in the raw number, you cannot make the assumption that they are all your friends and supporters, especially if the organization is in the midst of any kind of crisis or receiving negative media attention. Successful social media programs are successful because they turn audience members into advocates. Arriving at these metrics is what can really drive long-term success of the brand.

The metrics for social media should also have some connection with metrics in other operations. For example, if the success of social media is measured by sales calls generated, while the success of advertising campaigns is measured by completed sales, it is unclear which the organization values the most—the phone call or the sale. The answer would seem obvious. However, because organizations are just now establishing social media presence, they seem satisfied with the fact that people know they exist, ignoring the more important aspects of business operations.

Metrics Are Not Monitored

As with any other process, the establishment of metrics is useless without an accountability factor. All metrics must be developed with the assurance that they can be measured and the data is available. There are many things the organization would like to know about how social media is being used. However, that information may not be available (e.g., the data is not stored, the information was not considered part of the original design, the people designing the metrics do not understand how social media works, etc.).

The next risk is that the information is gathered but not disseminated. Closely related is the risk that no one individual or department has responsibility for reporting on and achieving the metrics. Depending on the governance structure, the responsible party can be anyone from the person who is doing the work to executive management. But responsibility for the success or failure of the metrics must be established.

This leads to the final point: There should be an escalation process to advise everyone when there is a significant departure from expected results. Remember, this plan should kick in if things are starting to turn bad or there is unexpected success. There are many stories out there about Web pages that almost succumbed to their own success—crashing or nearly crashing from volume. But crashing Web sites is the negative aspect of this success. If things are going better than expected, the organization should be advised when it is time to take advantage of such positive trends.

Metrics Drive Inappropriate Behavior

One last aspect of metrics is that you tend to get what you measure. So given enough incentive, people will make sure that they get what they are told to get. While this risk is often recognized by auditors working in sales departments (e.g., fictitious sales completed to achieve bonus levels), it has application in the social media area also. If a developer's bonus is based on hits per page and the numbers are lacking, he may be able to write a program that accesses that page as many times as necessary. If the promise was made that sales from Twitter feeds would increase, the responsible party may collude with the sales department to falsify the Twitter numbers.

These are relatively simplistic examples, but they illustrate that this risk is just as real an issue for social media as for other areas. In fact, because so many are still trying to understand how social media and the underlying programs work, it may be a bigger risk because the experts responsible for achieving the measures are often the ones who build the programs to record the measures. As noted before, much of this can be mitigated by ensuring that metrics actually match true measures of success and rewards are commensurate with the goals.

Inadequate Training

There are two aspects to this issue of training—the training of individuals involved in the development and content of social media, and the training of all employees on their roles and responsibilities. It might go without saying, but it is important that the people executing the program have an understanding of the tools they will be using. The worst-case scenario is an executive who must be trained on basic word processing protocols before he or she can provide input into a blog. (Even with something as simple as e-mail, some executives have had to be trained that all caps meant they were "yelling." Although, there is always the faint suspicion that they knew all along they were yelling.) It is important that everyone involved understands as much as possible about social media. Training should include a broad perspective of all social media as well as constant updates on new trends. It should also include some type of training on protocols within the blogosphere. For example, some people may need a refresher course on emoticons. Others may have picked up bad habits from their personal experience on the Internet, resulting in additional training regarding common courtesy.

Training should also be established to ensure all employees understand what the organization is doing with social networking and the role each of them plays. This should also include each employee's role outside the organization—how their personal interactions might have an impact on the organization.

Best practice is for the organization to announce its overall plans—what the social media strategy is and what it is trying to achieve. Then, as social media applications are rolled out, communications should go out explaining each stage and how it fits in with the overall plans. Also, as soon as the social networking policy is developed and approved, it should be reviewed with all personnel. Many organizations include this information in new employee indoctrination as part of the discussion of ethics and conflicts of interest policies. In addition, some repeat this training annually to ensure everyone is reminded of its importance.

Assigning the Wrong Personnel

We have talked a bit about the people who are actually in charge and responsible. However, the organization should also have a good understanding (either through established guidelines, job descriptions, or other documentation) of the type of people needed to accomplish the actual work. In worst-case scenarios, organizations have jumped into social media by assigning the task to the new intern (the suits didn't know anything about social networking so they gave it to one of the new kids). This means that the task of developing content and the conversation has been given to individuals with little or no experience with the business, the organization, or the common courtesies and protocols of business. However, it is similarly incorrect to assign individuals who have no concept of how social media communication works. In one situation, the individuals in charge of establishing a blog informed the bloggers they would be providing input once a month. This lack of knowledge about many of the basic tenets of blogging will doom the project from the start.

The selection of the executive or individuals to be charged with oversight is also integral to success. The best people to have in this role are those with a wide range of knowledge—understanding the basics of the technical needs, the way social media is used, the organization's culture and goals, and how to it all comes together in interacting with the public.

The Social Media Conversation Is Not Monitored

We have talked about monitoring many different aspects of social media from timelines for development to the metrics that measure success. However, the one area that may be most important is monitoring the conversations that are occurring. We already touched on this when we discussed the risk that the organization, after deciding not to participate, takes not continuing watching to see what is happening. But it is just as important to do so even if the organization has its own channels developed. To effectively monitor activity, it is very important to understand the full panoply of sites that make up social media. It is more than just Twitter and Facebook and blog conversations. You may need to determine what is out there on file sharing sites (YouTube or Flickr) or on customer service sites (Yelp, etc.) That does not mean you have to take action every time someone posts a photo of your company logo with a giant circle and hash mark over it. However, it does mean you need to recognize what is going on. Taking no action after an informed decision is what executives get the big bucks for; taking no action because of ignorance leads to failure.

More directly, the input being provided by the organization as well as the customers' responses should be monitored. For example, it might be expected that every blogger would be reviewing responses to his or her posts. However, if the CEO is the blogger, does he or she really have the time to look at every response? Who will review that conversation? What steps will be taken based on those responses? Very often the person tweeting or updating may not be focused on what else is occurring on those sites; they may see their job as posting information rather than worrying about responses. As noted in our discussion about regulatory risks, the actions that organizations take related to customer complaints can be regulated at the state or federal level—in some instances, starting the clock the minute the complaint is known by the organization. If someone posts a complaint to the Facebook page and no one is looking, the state is not going to accept that excuse.

One final aspect related to monitoring (and a significant risk in all aspects of social media) is the issue of posting proprietary or confidential material. As previously noted, social networking policies should spell out that such information should not be shared. But there are many opportunities and outlets for employees—current or former—to inappropriately post such information. This may require more specific searches and casting a broader net, but the loss of control of confidential materials is an important risk for the organization that must be considered.

Unprepared for Unexpected Responses

We already mentioned the risk of not being ready for a fire hose of response—that is, "better than we expected" metrics. But a more insidious issue crops up when communication with customers is expanded—they may not respond the way you expected them to. In fact, you can almost count on the conversation going in a different direction than you anticipated.

More than one corporate blog has disintegrated (some quite spectacularly) when respondents took the conversation in a different direction than expected. Wal-Mart, McDonald's, and Nestle have all had situations where they opened up blogs hoping to have friendly conversations about their products. However, rather than happy talks about how wonderful the products were and how people could find them, each was attacked by people using the blogs as an opportunity to express their displeasure with the social and corporate responsibility (or irresponsibility according to the bloggers) of those organizations. In at least two of those instances, the blogs did not survive.

If your organization opens the conversation, it should have contingency plans for when the conversation goes wrong (and it will go wrong). It is easy to say that you will address these when they occur, but this isn't like the old days. You do not have a week to contemplate the letter you received and structure a well-worded response. Instead, the complaint has gone across the world and you have minutes (if you are lucky, maybe an hour) before the rest of the world starts to play dog-pile on the rabbit—and you're the rabbit. Contingency does not mean having the answer, but it does mean ensuring that the person working that conversation has resources to help navigate the tricky waters. It may be access to legal or an executive or the head of public relations. But you don't want that part-time intern just trying to make up answers on his own. (This, too, is part of training that is important—recognizing when the conversation is veering, how to react in a politically sensitive way, and where to go for the right answers.)

Once you start monitoring all conversation, you may be surprised (not in a particularly good way) how much communication is going on about your organization. You also might find something equally surprising—that nobody is talking about your organization, but they love your competitors. Accordingly, just as you must be ready to handle the conversation that occurs on your sites, you must understand the other conversations going on to determine whether action is necessary.

Other General Risks

We have been focusing on risks that have particular importance when working with social media. However, it is important to

101

remember that many of the social media risks are the same general risks encountered in other parts of the organization.

Examples include vendor management (including assurance that the vendors used for social media meet the organization's requirements and that they can provide the services needed), contract management (including assurance that contracts have been reviewed and approved by the appropriate individuals), human resources (including assurance that job descriptions are properly developed, organization hiring and promotional practices are followed, and all employment records are maintained and filed), and expense management (including assurance that expenses are properly budgeted and approved).

> Social media is about sociology and psychology more than technology.
>
> —Brain Solis, Principal of FutureWorks
> and author of *Engage!*

It is worth speaking about IT risks separately. Most people assume this is a very important part of social media risks—and they are not wrong. However, any good reference can provide you with information on how to audit IT services and, in spite of the monumental changes social media has made for organizations, it does not represent a significant change in IT risks. The typical risks are there—secure servers, proper access (passwords, etc.), firewalls, backups, programming, and ability to retrieve data. The existing approaches to IT risk assessment and management can adequately address these concerns. You can find additional online resources about IT risks in Appendix A.

CHAPTER 6

Social Media Governance

Many interpretations exist about what constitutes "governance." Some see the governance role as being the responsibility of the boards of governors and related oversight committees. For purposes of discussing the role of governance in an organization's social media experience, we are going to use a much broader definition, looking at the various levels of governance, assurance, risk mitigation, control, and compliance issues.

Put another way, we look at governance as "who's watching the store." Beyond that we also consider who is building the store, who is running the store, and who is making sure the store is successful. Accordingly, in working through the aspects of governance (as we have just defined it) relating to the use of social media, we explore strategic, executive, and execution oversight, as well as the role of the assurance providers (e.g., internal auditing, risk management, compliance, and legal) in social media governance.

Boards of Directors

The highest level of corporate governance is usually located at the board of directors, board of governors, or other similar structure. The involvement of the board depends on the strategic impact of the organization's choices related to social media. In other words, if the organization has determined it is best to ignore or only stick a toe into the waters of social media, then there will be limited reporting to the board. If social media is to be a significant part of the organization's strategy, then the board should be fully apprised of the actions and associated risks (just as with any other strategic decisions). However, no matter which direction the organization chooses to take, it is still important to ensure the board is aware of the decisions, why these decisions were made, and the related risks.

It is important to reemphasize a point from Chapter 5. No matter the organization's involvement, education is needed about the role of social media and its impact on the organization at all levels—board, executive, management, and employee. If the board is to provide appropriate oversight related to the organization's social media decisions, it needs to have a good understanding of the state of social media as well as the associated risks and rewards.

Some board members are very social media savvy. However, no organization can take for granted their board is in that situation. Accordingly, time should be taken to ensure the board members are educated on such topics as the current state of social media (insuring they understand that it is more than tweeting and "friending"), the opportunities that exist, the regulatory issues related to the specific organization, the risks (whether the organization decides to participate or not), and, if not already articulated, the organization's direction related to social media. Depending on the temperament and knowledge of the board members, this information may be embraced as valuable, recognized as information they already had available, or dismissed as irrelevant (because the members still don't understand the impact). However, the conversation/education has to occur to ensure the board members have been kept up to date. Best practice is to ensure that the board is constantly updated.

Executive Oversight

The next level of oversight is at the executive level. This level represents where strategic decisions are made related to social media, including the alignment of social media strategies to the overall corporate strategies.

The primary responsibilities at this level are to ensure that the social media projects are moving as expected, they continue to be in alignment with overall strategies, significant risk issues or problems are brought to the executive's attention timely, and the overall objectives of the social media projects are being met. It may seem obvious, but there must be periodic communication to the executive level. Whether this is accomplished through executive committee updates, project management committees, or weekly or monthly information updates, there must be assurance that executive management understands the direction of social media projects to ensure they are in line with executive management's expectations.

Seldom are all executives kept abreast of the project's every step. It is at this level where a social media champion should exist—the executive who believes in what social media can accomplish and brings that story to other executives. The identification of this champion will say a lot about how seriously social media is taken and the direction it will go. In some instances, that champion can be the CEO. This shows that social media is a serious subject with a top priority. In many cases, because of the nature of social media, that executive champion will be in the sales or marketing arena. However, the champion may be from some other business line—product development, customer service, and the like. The important point is that a champion exists, someone who will be the torchbearer for the project in executive meetings and bring the message to the highest levels. That being said, there are three important issues to keep in mind when determining whether the governance structure related to executive oversight is adequate—having the wrong department in charge, an executive who does not believe or understand, and no one told us.

Having the Wrong Department in Charge

While there can technically be no "wrong department," the use of certain executives may be a warning that there is a misunderstanding of the role social media will play in the organization. In particular, if such executives as the chief risk officer (CRO), chief compliance officer (CCO), or chief legal counsel are charged with overseeing social media, this may be an indicator that there is too much emphasis on the risks and negative aspects of social media.

Similarly (and surprisingly), the use of the chief information officer (CIO) can be an indicator that there is a misunderstanding of the risks and opportunities related to social media. In some situations, because the organization sees computers being used, they put the IT department on the job. Again, this misses the point of social media. It is not an IT function; it is a communication function.

With all that being said, it is not necessarily wrong to have any of these individuals responsible for social media. Often, the most important thing is just having an executive responsible who sees the full benefits of social media, understands how it aligns to the organization's strategies, and believes in its ultimate benefits. However, because of the nature of their roles and responsibilities, the individuals in these (and similar) positions may not be conducive to successful implementation and the sustainability of social media strategies.

An Executive Who Does Not Believe or Understand

As discussed, the executive who is appointed to oversee the organization's social media activities has to believe in the need and success of such programs. You will note the continued use of the word "champion" in this discussion. As with any project, if there is not a champion—someone who believes in the project—then the chance of the initiative's survival in executive sessions becomes questionable. Without an advocate, the ultimate death can occur—a lack of resource allocation.

The next worst issue is when the executive does not understand the full risks and rewards of social media. Just as the board must be educated, executives should be educated on what is going on, how it can benefit the organization, and on the full regalia of risks that exists. While those involved in social media projects can be those educators, there must be someone at the executive level who understands this to ensure that social media is properly represented at executive meetings and decisions affecting social media are properly communicated downward.

No One Told Us

The ultimate concern at the executive level is that there be at least one executive who knows that social media work is going on within the organization. Because social media is so new and so fast moving, it is very easy for a department to take it upon itself to enter the arena. They are moving quickly and may not have time for all the necessary protocols, which include making sure executive management knows what is happening. They are so excited that they are telling everyone; it's just that "everyone" does not include the executives. This is not done with malicious intent. It is just that the important detail of informing executive management has slipped through the cracks. Accordingly, through whatever method they can find, executives need to ensure that they know what social media the organization is taking on, communicate with each other to ensure the entire group knows, and (coming full circle) make sure an executive has been appointed to provide guidance and governance.

Project/Process/Tactical Oversight

Most of the oversight responsibilities we have discussed up to now (board and executive oversight) have been related to strategic issues. The organization also must have in place, at some level, oversight responsibilities related to the tactical issues. The actual structure for oversight depends on the size of the initiative, as well as the type of organization, the organization's structure, and the resources that are being allocated. In some instances, a series of committees may be responsible. In other instances, the department charged with development may be sufficient to provide the oversight. For purposes of our discussion, we will talk in terms of various committees. However, the tasks can be taken on within any structure.

No matter the situation, responsibility should be spelled out for the right person, department, or committee, and reporting responsibilities established to ensure that progress, issues, and high-level decision making are properly elevated. The important point is that these things are accomplished at some level so that executive management knows what is occurring.

Committee Makeup/Department Feedback

Whether oversight is through a committee or accomplished as part of the departmental structure, there needs to be assurance that feedback is received from all possible areas. For social media, it is important to ensure feedback and involvement from:

- Legal
- Communications/Public Relations
- Compliance/Regulatory
- Risk
- Marketing
- Other Operational Functions
- Human Resources
- IT

Yes, it is just about every department within the organization. However, this reemphasizes the point that social media should be acting as the voice of the organization, and that means there should be assurance that all parts of the organization understand what is going on. This also helps ensure that no department is going off on its own. The public relations and marketing departments are included because there should be alignment in the message between social media and these departments. Departments such as risk, compliance, IT, and human resources should be involved because their roles include ensuring the organization keeps out of trouble in their respective areas. And legal is involved because legal just seems to need to be involved in everything.

A Warning to Committee Members

When recruiting and working with the committee members, it is important that they be constantly reminded that this is not a normal project and not a normal process. Many of them will be more familiar with standard processes and standard projects, maybe even coming from a production or manufacturing environment. However, social media is a completely different animal; it is about information planning. That is, rather than being concerned with the way things are done, this committee will be concerned with the way information is gathered and disseminated. Even people who think they are used to this type of conversation (e.g., marketing) may have to go through a paradigm shift before they make good decisions.

Roles and Responsibilities

The committee should establish an understanding of the roles and responsibilities of all parties. If there is more than one committee, the differences in their responsibilities should be clearly established. For example, a technical committee might have been established. Such a title leaves unclear whether their responsibilities are limited to computer technologies or might include determination of the actual media outlets. This latter interpretation could be in conflict with an operational committee. Establishing these responsibilities and, just as important, aligning them will help reduce overlap and confusion. Also, an overall analysis of all responsibilities should be accomplished to ensure that no responsibilities have been missed.

One other point: the more committees that have been assigned varying responsibilities and the more people who are involved, the more it is necessary to establish a coordinating committee—that is, a committee to ensure all objectives, work, risks, and so forth are aligned and included.

Objectives

Whether oversight is accomplished by a committee or department, and whether social media is seen as an individual project or a continuing role, objectives must be established to understand what will be achieved. These objectives should articulate what is to be accomplished and how, in broad terms, it will be accomplished.

Objectives related to social media should outline how the organization's social media presence will be developed (if not already in place), how it will be maintained, the periodic reevaluations that will occur, and that the changes will be accomplished as necessary. This should include reference to the overall organizational strategies and show the alignment of social media approaches to the organization's strategies and objectives.

While the actual media to be used might be included in the objectives, the constant change in this arena will mean the constant updating of the objectives. Although reviewing and updating objectives is an important consideration (see below), constant revisions can be confusing. As an example, think of the objective that could have been written indicating the department will increase the organization's visibility on Friendster. That's an objective that is ripe for change.

An objective statement for any organization should also include a reference to monitoring social media. This objective needs to include reference to all types of social media, not just be limited to that which is sponsored by the organization. As discussed in Chapter 3, even if the organization is not involved in social media, there is a wide variety of areas where the organization may be exposed, and such monitoring must exist. (Note that, even if the organization is not involved, there is the need for a tactical oversight level related to social media.)

There are two other important aspects of objectives that are true in all situations, but may be even more important in a social media environment. The first is that the objectives should be constantly updated. As we have noted many times, the world of social media is changing quickly. That means that, in short order, the concepts and objectives that have been established may be outdated. Think in terms of an objective that is built around an organization using blogs to deliver its message. This would be a strategy based on relatively large blocks of information being delivered daily. Today, there is still a role for such delivery, but the instantaneous 140-character deliveries are becoming more and more important, and the organization's tactical objectives may need to change accordingly.

The second aspect is the need for objectives to be reviewed at all levels—both up to the executive level and down to the employee level. At the highest levels, the review of social media objectives is important to ensure alignment with the organization's other strategies (as we have said many times before) and to ensure that executives are current on the latest developments of this fast-moving area. A review with all employees is also important. It will ensure they understand what the organization is trying to achieve, and they can often be the source of information on recent changes to the social media environment. In addition, it reinforces their responsibilities related to social media.

Requirements

Underlying the objectives are the requirements of the social media project. Requirements can fall into many categories. For social media, this includes such aspects as the specific systems that will be used, the specific media (note that this is more detailed than objectives, is changed more often, and, accordingly, includes the actual tools being used), and what is expected of those systems. Depending on the project, this can also include such things as specific skill needs for people doing the work, the time frames for feedback from decision-making committees, and even response times from media providers. In other words, it is the requirements of what the team needs to achieve its objectives.

Task Definition

Related to the establishment of objectives, roles, and responsibilities, every committee should establish the specific tasks that will be accomplished. This drives to the very meaning of tactical. The individual tasks represent the specific actions that will be taken to accomplish objectives. This should include identifying, if possible, the person responsible for individual steps, processes, or tasks. At the very least, the lead of the unit responsible should be identified along with the activity.

Develop Measures of Success

Having defined the objectives, the next thing to determine is how to ensure those objectives have been met. In addition, proof is needed to show that the investment of time, money, and people has been of value to the organization.

In Chapter 3, we discussed many of the various metrics that can be established, and in Chapter 5, we discussed some of the related risks. Ensuring that the risk of poor metrics is properly mitigated is the responsibility of committees established at this level. This is an important component of tactical oversight; determining and getting agreement on (by executive management) the indicators that show success.

There is one other point to be made about social media measures of success. Even with the growing popularity of social media and the increased realization by management that it is an important aspect of business, there may still be reluctance to devoting lots of resources to these projects. Identifying the proper timelines and measures of success—and meeting them—can become strong motivators to reluctant management that the right things are being done and more investment will result in more success.

Prioritizations

Tactical oversight includes responsibility for prioritizing social media projects and resource use. There are a lot of opportunities out there, and your organization will not be able to take advantage of all of them. The first prioritization relates to what media will be used—blogs, microblogging, video sharing, and so on. Such a prioritization will be based on the skills of the people involved and, as usual, the resources available.

Similarly, allocation of the resources has to be prioritized. If there is one great writer on staff and two who are not so great, a determination needs to be made as to where the best content (the best writer) should be placed. As always, prioritization includes determining where to spend the limited money that is being given.

As with so many other aspects, this prioritization should be revisited often. Like the example used earlier, if you made Friendster your priority a while ago, that should have been revisited and probably changed. Such prioritization reviews and changes should be closely entwined with the reviews of objectives.

Legal, Compliance, and Risk Assessments

We have already discussed the involvement of the various assurance providers. However, it is the committee's responsibility to take the recommendations of these departments and ensure that they are appropriately implemented. Every industry has its own issues and every regulatory body seems to be working overtime trying to figure out what is going on in social media, establishing new rules and regulations. Input from these providers is invaluable to keeping the organization out of trouble.

Issue Elevation

While implied in many of the previous items, it is worth specifically mentioning that there should be a process for the quick evaluation of potential roadblocks to progress. When identified, there should be a similarly quick evaluation to determine the severity of the issue. Finally, a method should be in place that, based on the severity of the issue, establishes a hierarchy for elevating these issues. In other words, how to get to the right person, how to get the problem solved without going too high, and when to let executives know when the objectives are in trouble.

Statement of Direction

All this information should be leading to written documentation that ensures everyone involved understands the roles and responsibilities, objectives, and purpose of the project, committee, or department. For committees or project management, this is usually accomplished with a charter. For a department, it may be outlined in a departmental purpose and objective statement. (In some instances, visions or missions can be established. However, these are often insufficient to properly outline the expectations.) No matter the structure, this document should include many of the areas we have been discussing, including what is to be accomplished and how success will be measured. It also should include the issues that are being addressed, the scope of work, and the business objectives.

Assurance Providers

Just as there are many interpretations of governance, there are also many interpretations of "assurance providers." For this discussion, we use a three-level approach to understanding assurance. The first level is the work that is done by the department itself. That is, how does the department ensure that things are going right, such as quality assurance, approvals, and so forth? The second level of assurance is that provided by departments with specific areas of concern—areas where the organization sees a specific need to have additional oversight. Generally, these are such areas as risk, compliance, and Sarbanes-Oxley-related activities. The third level is the assurance provided by individuals providing more advisory-type assurance—legal, internal auditing, and the external auditors. A quality governance structure includes all these participants working together to provide broad assurance.

For social media, the first line of defense is exemplified by various aspects. The first is the metrics used to ensure that the department is achieving its objectives. It is also expected that reviews are completed related to the actual construction of any sites or projects.

However, the biggest issue is probably how the organization ensures that the appropriate message is being sent out. Depending on the activity and availability of resources, this can mean the review of every correspondence, or a representative sample. As an example, while some bloggers are given the freedom by their organizations to post directly, others have a review process whereby the blogger submits the blog and it is reviewed (by an editor, supervisor, etc.) and posted, edited, or rejected.

Such close scrutiny tends to affect the spontaneity of blogging and can mean a posting is outdated before it even hits the site. In addition, such scrutiny is much harder in a microblog (e.g., Twitter) environment. In those situations, the department should establish a post-posting review. It will depend on the sensitivity of the area whether this is constant monitoring or a random review. (Of course, some of that is decided by the volume. It is easy to monitor everything if there is only one post daily.)

Also within that first line of defense is the review of non-organization sites. This is usually a combination of those assigned to review sites and the use of software that looks for keywords. However, it is also worth pointing out that all employees can help in this endeavor. This is one of the great values of allowing employees access to all sites. In this way, the entire organization works to be a first line of defense.

Whether every entry is reviewed or only some are reviewed, there will be a situation where things are not going as the organization had planned. As mentioned previously, the organization should have established contingency plans to handle this. Whether it is trying to ignore or control the conversation, or if it is the nuclear option of shutting down the site, the first line of defense should include such contingency plans.

The second line of defense includes such groups as risk and compliance. While the focus of these departments is not specifically on social media, they should ensure that their plans include determining their potential role in reviewing operations. We have already indicated that risk and compliance groups should be part of the committees established over social media to ensure their concerns are addressed right away. However, as social media is used in the organization, such groups should also look at what is going on to make sure there are still no problems. Those individuals or groups in charge of social media should invite them in whenever there is an indication of potential issues, but risk and compliance departments should also build into their schedule periodic reviews to ensure things continue to run smoothly.

The final line of defense can be thought of as being available to provide advice and assurance when requested (by either the department or higher levels of management). Of course, both internal and external auditors should include social media as part of their risk analyses to determine the audit activities that should exist. (Also, while not listed in any of the previous committees, it is a good idea to have some representation from auditing to give advice on risk and control activities.) Similarly, legal should be available to offer advice on any legal aspects that may arise. Legal should also be proactive—watching for and identifying new legal issues that might affect the operation of the organization's social media staff.

CHAPTER 7

The Social Media Audit

Following is a sample audit program that can be used in reviewing a company's social media activities. Broad areas of review have been identified. For each area we have also provided the objective of the tests related to that area, some general documents which might be reviewed, various audit steps to support the objective, and the purposes of the audit step. In building this audit program, we have made a few assumptions.

The first is that the reader is working in an environment where a basic audit approach already exists. Accordingly, this is not a comprehensive audit program and does not include such basic steps as notifying management that the audit will be taking place, preparing an initial information request, clearing review notes, or scheduling a meeting to review results. Rather, it focuses on the reviews and tests that might be included.

The second is that the organization under review has a comprehensive structure—board of directors, oversight committees, and so on. If that is not the case, the auditor should recognize the purpose of the function being reviewed and verify that this purpose is similarly accomplished within the alternate structure.

Third, this program is designed for an organization that is planning to fully participate in social media. If the organization under review has determined it will not participate in an area described in this chapter, the auditor must decide whether it is an area that is critical to the control structure. For example, deciding to refrain from participation in social media is a strategic decision. While the auditor may not agree, it is not an issue (as long as there is appropriate documentation related to the decision). However, determining that metrics will not be needed is a control issue and should be reported accordingly.

Finally, in Chapter 5 we discussed that there are some risks that, while still important, are not significantly different when considered in a social media environment (e.g., vendor management, human resources, or contract management). Similarly, we have not included specific audit steps for these areas. Speaking specifically to potential IT audit areas, the steps are not significantly different than would be completed in any review of IT processes. Again, we refer readers to the many other valuable texts in this area (see Appendix A).

Social Media Governance and Oversight

Objective: To determine whether effective oversight has been established for the use of all social media, including social media specifically developed by the organization.

Documents for Review:	Meeting Notes – Board of Directors
	Meeting Notes – Senior Management
	Meeting Notes – Social Media Committees
	Charter, Purpose, Objectives – Social Media Committees
	Meeting Notes – Committees with potential social media implications

Audit Step	Purpose
Review board of directors' meeting notes to determine their involvement and to ensure the board of directors has been:	Provided information on the risks and opportunities related to social media.
	Advised of the organization's strategy related to social media.
	Appropriately involved in significant decisions related to social media.
	Updated, at least annually, on the status of social media initiatives.
Interview senior executives to determine their involvement in social media oversight and to ensure they have been:	Provided information on the risks and opportunities related to social media.
	Involved in decisions related to the organization's strategy related to social media.
	Appropriately updated on the status of individual projects and the overall social media strategy.
	Involved in assuring alignment of the social media strategy with corporate strategies.

(*Continued*)

Social Media Governance and Oversight (*Continued*)

Review social media committee charters, purpose, objectives, and related documentation to ensure:	At least one individual at the executive management level has been assigned responsibility for the committee.
	The charter, purpose, and objectives have been appropriately reviewed and approved by executive management.
	One committee has been given responsibility for oversight if more than one committee is responsible for various aspects of social media.
	Roles and responsibilities have been properly identified and assigned.
	Approval and escalation policies have been established and followed.
Review social media committee documentation to determine:	Whether the individual selected as committee chair has the appropriate credentials (e.g., appropriate skill set, appropriate authority, etc.).
	Whether the committee has included the appropriate departments.
	Whether the appropriate committee members have been assigned (e.g., those who are at the appropriate level in the organization, have an understanding of social media opportunities and risks, are from the appropriate departments).
	Whether procedures are in place in the event a member is unable to participate or must leave the committee.
	Whether information related to the committee has been appropriately shared with executive management, departmental management, and other committees.

What periodic reviews exist to ensure the committee makes appropriate mid-course corrections.

Whether the strategy and plans for social media are in alignment with corporate goals and objectives.

What steps have been taken to identify all social media initiatives that might be occurring throughout the organization.

What steps have been taken to prioritize competing projects and the use of limited resources.

Whether completion timelines have been established and updates provided.

Whether the committee has appropriately reached out to risk and compliance-related functions such as legal, compliance, regulatory affairs, risk, or internal auditing.

Additional Tests:	Review committee meeting minutes for all committees. Verify that all committees with social media impact have been reported to the social media committees and senior management.
	Review social media committee meeting minutes to identify potential issues and opportunities. Verify that these have been properly escalated.
	Conduct a survey of employees to determine their involvement in social media, including working on social media initiatives for the organization. Verify that these have been recognized by the social media committee.

Social Media Strategy

Objective: To determine whether a social media strategy has been developed that is complete, aligned with other corporate strategies, and appropriately communicated.

Documents for Review:	Social Media Strategy
	Organization Strategy, Goals, and Objectives
	Meeting Notes – Board of Directors
Review the social media strategy to ensure:	It is in alignment with the organization's strategy and objectives.
	It appropriately addresses all known channels.
	All stakeholders have been considered (not just customer service and sales).
	It includes reference to the message and image the organization wishes to communicate.
	The appropriate target markets, the desired relationships, the desired conversational engagement, and how stakeholders will use social media have all been included.
Additional Tests:	Review documentation at the executive and board level to ensure the strategy has been appropriately reviewed and approved.

Social Media Plan

Objective: To determine whether the organization's planning related to social media is complete, in alignment with the related strategies, and appropriately communicated.

Documents for Review:	Social Media Plan
	Social Media Strategy
	Organization Strategy, Plans, Objectives, and Goals
	Charter, Purpose, Objectives – Social Media Committees
	Vendor Contracts and Agreements
	Vendor Correspondence
Through discussion and review of appropriate documents, verify that plans related to social media include:	Goals that are specific, measurable, achievable, relevant, and time bound.
	The social media channels that will be used.
	How the stakeholders will be engaged, including the style, frequency, and consistency of the messages.
	The departments or individuals that will be responsible for various portions of the plan.
	Applicable limitations on the plan (restricted channels, resource constraints, etc.).
	Allotment of resources necessary to achieve the objectives.

(Continued)

Social Media Plan (*Continued*)

Review social media plans to ensure:	They are in alignment with the organization's objectives, goals, and plans. The plans are in alignment with the social media strategy, including the chosen channels, target markets, and communication styles.
Identify any vendors being used to help support social media projects. Review any contracts and communications to ensure:	Appropriate service-level agreements have been established. Clear measures of success have been determined. Quality assurance procedures have been developed related to work produced by the vendor.
Additional Tests:	Compare goals with the current status of the project. If any gaps exist, verify that these have been properly elevated. Review vendor service-level agreements and measures of success, comparing them to the current status of the project. If they are not being met, verify that the issues have been properly elevated. Analyze expense payments toward identifying vendors potentially working on social media. Verify that these have been identified and that appropriate agreements are in place.

Plan Execution

Objective: To determine whether appropriate policies and procedures have been implemented to ensure the successful execution of the social media plan.

Documents for Review:	Organization charts
	Job Descriptions
	Departmental Procedures – Social Media
	Employee Experience Backgrounds
	Required Metrics
	Employee Performance Plans
	Quality Assurance Procedures
Review organization charts for those departments involved with social media to ensure:	Proper reporting relationships exist within the department.
	Appropriate oversight exists within each department.
Review job descriptions for those involved in social media projects to ensure:	The appropriate job skills have been identified.
	Education requirements match the needs of the project.
	Appropriate supervision and oversight has been established.
Through discussion with personnel and reviews of related documents, ensure that:	All applicable departments have been provided with the organization's social media strategy, direction, and plans.
	Roles and responsibilities have been defined for all individuals working on social media projects.

(Continued)

Plan Execution (*Continued*)

Individuals working on social media initiatives have the proper experience and knowledge.

Appropriate supervision has been established within each department. (This may be cross-referenced to the tests on monitoring.)

Metrics have been established for each applicable department. (This may be cross-referenced to the tests on metrics.)

Appropriate quality assurance procedures have been established over the work completed.

Additional Tests:

Review the education and background of individuals involved in social media. Match these to job descriptions or other requirements that have been established for the position. If there is a mismatch, verify that appropriate follow-up is being taken (e.g., additional training).

Review performance plans for employees involved in social media to verify that these plans are in alignment with the goals and objectives of social media initiatives.

Review quality assurance documentation. In the event issues were identified in the reviews, verify that these were properly escalated.

Metrics

Objective: To determine whether metrics have been established to ensure successful implementation and use of social media.

Documents for Review:	Required Metrics
	Policies and Procedures – Metrics
	Metrics Result Reports
	Documentation of Issue Escalation
Review records related to metrics, including procedures, reports, and actions taken, to ensure:	Metrics have been established.
	The metrics established are measurable.
	The metrics have value to the department or organization.
	Metrics align to the organization's strategy, goals, or objectives.
	Metrics align to the social media strategy, goals, or objectives.
	Metrics include a definition of acceptable ranges, including an indication when additional action may be required.
	Responsibility for gathering metrics has been established, including gathering and reporting.
	Appropriate action is taken when metrics are not within acceptable ranges.
Additional Tests:	Review recent metrics results to ensure that the data within the department matches that reported to the committees and executive management.

(*Continued*)

Metrics (*Continued*)

Extract data that is used for the metrics. Perform an analysis to verify that the metrics in the departmental reports match the actual data.

Review metrics results for potential issues. If identified, verify these were appropriately elevated.

Monitoring

Objective: To determine whether appropriate monitoring systems have been established over communications related to social media.

Documents for Review:	Policies and Procedures – Monitoring
	Documentation of Issue Escalation
Through discussions with personnel and reviews of documentation, ensure:	Plans are in place to appropriately monitor social media, including content developed by the organization.
	Areas (keywords, hot topics, restricted issues) have been identified and are included in all monitoring activities.
	Reviews exist to identify appropriate monitoring tools.
	Identified tools are consistently used.
	Plans have been established to handle situations requiring increased scrutiny.
	Guidelines exist for the handling of sensitive or problem issues.
	Escalation procedures exist to allow timely responses from the appropriate level.
	Responses to identified issues are handled as quickly as desired.
Additional Tests:	Review organization sponsored social media. If any issues are identified, determine whether these were included as part of the organization's monitoring.
	Using social media monitoring tools, perform checks for keywords that match those used by the organization. Verify that items identified in the auditor's review match information reported from the organization's monitoring systems.

Training

Objective: To determine whether appropriate levels of training have been established to ensure all personnel have been provided sufficient information regarding the organization's approach, policies, and procedures related to social media.

Documents for Review:	Training Materials – Social Media
	Training Materials – Potentially Related to Social Media
	Policies and Procedures – Training
	Training Plans
	Training Schedules
	Training Records
Review all training materials to ensure:	All appropriate areas are covered, including the current state of social media, opportunities and risks related to the use of social media, the direction the organization is taking, and the social media policy.
	Specific training exists for the special needs of different areas (e.g., board of director members versus line personnel).
Through discussion and review of additional documentation, ensure that:	One department is ultimately responsible for assuring the achievement of training goals.
	All social media training needs have been identified, both general needs related to all personnel and specific needs for individual employees.
	Plans exist for updating training as necessary.
	Plans exist to provide refresher courses on social media.

	Other training (for example, training on the code of ethics) includes issues related to social media.
Review training records to ensure:	Training schedules have been established for all personnel, including executive management and the board of directors.
	Completion of the training is documented.
	All personnel have gone through all required levels of training.
Additional Tests:	Survey employees to determine whether training was received. Ensure this matches documentation upon completion of training.

Social Media Policy

Objective: To determine whether a social media policy has been developed and communicated which provides (internally) direction related to employees' use of all social media and (externally) guidance to external stakeholders using the organization's social media outlets.

Documents for Review:	Internal Social Media Policy
	External Social Media Policy
	Training Schedule
	Meeting Notes – Board of Directors
	Meeting Notes – Social Media Committees
	Communication of Policy to Departments

Through discussion and reviews of documentation, ensure that:	All applicable committees have been involved in the establishment of the policy.
	All applicable departments (particularly legal and human resources) have been involved in the establishment of the policy.
	The policy has been properly reviewed and approved.
	Training specific to the social media policy has been delivered (cross-reference to training above).
	The external social media policy has been published on all organization-sponsored social media.
	The policies available on different organization-sponsored social media are in alignment.

138

Review the internal social media policy to ensure it includes:	Alignment with other corporate policies (for example, code of ethics, restrictions on proprietary information, etc.).
	Acceptable social media practices.
	The steps the organization will take for noncompliance.
	The organization's right to monitor employees' activities.
	What the organization will allow nonemployees to do on organization-sponsored sites.
	Guidelines for communication (e.g., adding value to the dialogue, using a conversational tone, treating all with respect, etc.).
	A statement on ownership of posted materials.
	Limitations related to endorsement of products and services.
Review the external social media policy to ensure it includes:	How the organization will monitor activities.
	How the organization will respond to various input.
	Other sites maintained by the organization.
	Service-level agreements related to inquiries from stakeholders.
Additional Tests:	Review organization-sponsored sites to verify that external social media policies have been appropriately posted.

Regulatory and Compliance

Objective: To determine whether the organization's actions related to social media comply with all applicable federal and local regulatory issues.

Documents for Review:	Risk Assessments
	Updates on Regulatory Changes
Through discussion with the appropriate departments and review of supporting documentation, determine whether:	Risk assessments conducted at all levels of the organization include consideration of social media risks.
	Results of risk assessments related to social media are appropriately elevated to the responsible committee.
	Organization-wide reviews of changes in laws and regulations include consideration of social media.
	Results of reviews over regulations and laws related to social media are appropriately elevated to the responsible committee.
Additional Tests:	Review known changes to laws and regulations related to social media. Verify that these were appropriately elevated as part of the organization's review.

APPENDICES

Chapter Links

Throughout this book are numerous references to Web sites, social networking platforms and tools, people, techno-jargon, research studies, and some really relevant quotes. In order to get the most out of the book, the authors wanted to share as much as possible and created this appendix to not only act as a reference for specific sources of information but to also provide readers with an aggregated source of additional information and insight that might be useful in the professional or personal quest for additional information on social media.

And since the social media space moves so quickly, the authors will be providing additional information and references over time on www.auditingsocialmedia.com.

Chapter 1   Social Media: An Overview

Computerized Bulletin Board System and Wade Christensen
    en.wikipedia.org/wiki/CBBS
Mike Volpe quote: Where is Social Media Now (PG version)
    www.slideshare.net/mzkagan/what-is-social-media-now-
    4747765 (slide 57)
AOL.com
    www.aol.com

AOL Instant Messenger

www.aim.com

SixDegrees.com: Early social networking platform

en.wikipedia.org/wiki/SixDegrees.com

Open Diary: A blogging platform

www.opendiary.com

Live Journal: A blogging/online community platform

www.livejournal.com

Blogger: A blogging platform

www.blogger.com/start

Friendster: A social networking platform

www.friendster.com

Linkedin.com: A professional social networking platform

www.linkedin.com

Wordpress: A blogging platform

www.wordpress.com (hosted version); www.wordpress
.org (downloadable version)

Widget: Expanded definition

en.wikipedia.org/wiki/Web_widget

Delicious.com: Social bookmarking site

www.delicious.com

Folksonomy: Expanded definition

en.wikipedia.org/wiki/Folksonomy

RSS 2.0: Real Simple Syndication

cyber.law.harvard.edu/rss/rss.html

MySpace.com: Social networking platform

www.myspace.com

Flickr.com: A photo and video sharing social network platform
  www.flickr.com

Facebook.com: A social networking platform
  www.facebook.com

Royal Pingdom: Study—Ages of social network users
  royal.pingdom.com/2010/02/16/study-ages-of-social-
  network-users

Yelp: A local consumer review social networking platform
  www.yelp.com

YouTube: A video social networking platform
  www.youtube.com

Twitter: A microblogging platform
  www.twitter.com

bit.ly: A link shortening tool, ideal for incorporating into tweets
  bit.ly

Twitter Search
  search.twitter.com

Best Buy's Twelpforce: Best Buy's customer service program
  using Twitter
  twitter.com/#!/TWELPFORCE

Dell's Dell Direct Outlet
  twitter.com/#!/delloutlet

Apple's App Store for iPhone
  www.apple.com/iphone/apps-for-iphone/#heroOverview

Location-based Service: Expanded definition
  en.wikipedia.org/wiki/Location-based_service

Popular Location-based Service Applications:
  - Foursquare: www.foursquare.com
  - GoWalla: www.gowalla.com

- WeReward: www.wereward.com
- Locational Privacy information www.pleaserobme.com

Deloitte 2009 Ethics & Workplace Survey

www.deloitte.com/view/en_US/us/About/Ethics-Independence/8aa3cb51ed812210VgnVCM100000ba42f00aRCRD.htm

Foreward to Crossing the Chasm (author, Geoffery Moore) by Regis McKenna

www.amazon.com/Crossing-Chasm-Marketing-Technology-Mainstream/dp/1841120634

Chapter 2   Social Media: A Corporate Strategy

Social Media: Embracing the Opportunities, Averting the Risks, by Russell Herder and Ethos Business Law

www.russellherder.com/SocialMediaResearch

Zynga: Social gaming developer of Farmville and Mafia Wars

www.zynga.com

80% of U.S. adults use social networks

www.forrester.com/rb/Research/broad_reach_of_social_technologies/q/id/55132/t/2

Kelly Feller quote: Korn Ferry Institute – Social Media Gets to Work

www.kornferryinstitute.com/about_us/by_industry/functional_specialty/information_technology_officer/publication/2325/Social_media

Mark Zuckerberg: Founder of Facebook.com

www.facebook.com/markzuckerberg

Bonin Bough: Global Director of Digital and Social Media, PepsiCo

www.businessinsider.com/pepsis-secrets-to-social-media-strategy-2010–8

Dell's use of social media: ENGAGEMENTdb by Altimeter Group and WetPaint

engagementdb.com

Charlene Li and Josh Bernoff: 2007 *Social Technographics*

forrester.typepad.com/groundswell/2007/04/forresters_
new_.html

2010 Update to *Social Technographics* by Josh Bernoff and Ted Schadler

forrester.typepad.com/groundswell/2010/01/conversation
alists-get-onto-the-ladder.html

CoTweet: An enterprise-level Twitter management platform

www.cotweet.com

Quote from Joshua-Michele Ross in 2009 *Forbes* article: "A Corporate Guide for Social Media"

www.forbes.com/2009/06/30/social-media-guidelines-
intelligent-technology-oreilly.html

Stefanie Nelson: former manager of @DellOutlet for Dell

twitter.com/#!/stefanieatdell

Dell Outlet surpasses US $2 million in sales on Twitter

en.community.dell.com/dell-blogs/Direct2Dell/b/direct-
2dell/archive/2009/06/11/delloutlet-surpasses-2-million-
on-twitter.aspx

Dell's Twitter accounts

www.dell.com/twitter

Jerry Maguire: the movie

www.imdb.com/title/tt0116695

Microsoft's Most Valuable Professional (MVP) program

mvp.support.microsoft.com

Sodexo USA Careers: Network with Us

www.sodexousa.com/usen/careers/network/network.asp

MyStarbucksIdea.com

  mystarbucksidea.force.com

Salesforce.com

  www.salesforce.com

Will It Blend?

  www.willitblend.com

BlendTec: Blenders Used in Will It Blend?

  blendtec.com

Cone 2009 New Media Study

  www.coneinc.com/news/request.php?id=2614

Altimeter Group: Social Strategy: Getting your company ready by Jeremiah Owyang (organizational structure starts on slide 22) www.slideshare.net/CIC_China/ social-strategy-getting-your-company-ready

Chapter 3   Monitoring and Measuring

John Hayes quote, PriceWaterhouseCoopers: How consumer conversation will transform business

  www.pwc.com/en_GX/gx/technology-media-convergence/pdf/consumertransformbusiness.pdf

Charlene Li quote

  smartblogs.com/socialmedia/2010/03/22/charlene-li-on-social-media-and-leadership

SocialMention.com: A free social media monitoring tool

  www.socialmention.com

Anthony van der Hoek quote: PricewaterhouseCoopers: How consumer conversation will transform business

  www.pwc.com/en_GX/gx/technology-media-convergence/pdf/consumertransformbusiness.pdf

Dell's customer-generated idea platform

  www.ideastorm.com

Michael Troiano quote: Where Is Social Media Now (PG version)
www.slideshare.net/mzkagan/what-is-social-media-now
-4747765 (slide 58)

Chapter 4   Social Media Policies

Social Media: Embracing the Opportunities, Averting the Risks,
by Russell Herder and Ethos Business Law
www.russellherder.com/SocialMediaResearch

Deloitte 2009 Ethics & Workplace Survey
www.deloitte.com/view/en_US/us/About/Ethics-
Independence/8aa3cb51ed812210VgnVCM100000
ba42f00aRCRD.htm

Zappos.com: Example of company that has embedded social
media into its corporate culture
www.zappos.com

Federal Trade Commission: Guidelines Governing Endorsements,
Testimonials
www.ftc.gov/opa/2009/10/endortest.shtm

Air Force Crisis Communications Chart
www.wired.com/dangerroom/2009/01/usaf-blog-respo

Social Media Training Programs:
- Word of Mouth Marketing Association: www.womma.org
- Social Media Club via local chapters: www.socialmediaclub
.org

Chapter 5   Social Media Risks

Deloitte 2009 Ethics & Workplace Survey
www.deloitte.com/view/en_US/us/About/Ethics-
Independence/8aa3cb51ed812210VgnVCM100000
ba42f00aRCRD.htm

Julia Roy quote: Where is Social Media Now (PG version)
www.slideshare.net/mzkagan/what-is-social-media-now
-4747765 (slide 62)

Social Media Issues—Not Prepared for Unexpected Responses:

- Wal-Mart: Blazing a Trail to Distrust (2006): www.imedia connection.com/content/11814.asp
- Motrin Bows to Social Media Pressure from Moms: www .readwriteweb.com/archives/motrin_bows_to_social_media_pr.php
- Nestle Incites Social Media Mob after Greenpeace Campaign: econsultancy.com/us/blog/5625-nestle-fails-to-tame-the-social-media-mob
- Brian Solis quote: 49 lines from 23 Sources about Social Media: socialsteve.wordpress.com/2010/08/15/49-lines-from-23-sources-about-social-media

IT Risks

- Texts on IT Audits and Risks: www.theiia.org/bookstore/department/technology-10022.cfm?
- Global Technology Audit Guides (GTAG): www.theiia .org/guidance/technology

Appendix B

2007 Comscore/Kelsey Research study
www.comscore.com/Press_Events/Press_Releases
/2007/11/Online_Consumer_Reviews_Impact_Offline_
Purchasing_Behavior

Common and Popular Social Media Tools and Platforms

The challenge of finding the best social media tools is that there are so many out there. With each one being a little different than the others, the decision to pick the best can be a time-consuming, yet important endeavor. The selection of tools, and along with it the use of social media within an organization, requires focus and the strict effort to avoid the "shiny object syndrome" and head for the latest new thing that comes along. Such attempts often end up as inconsistent and half-hearted efforts that confuse your stakeholders. It is important that the organization applies a focused, strategic view of social media and chooses the right tools to implement the strategy as discussed throughout this book.

The next sections feature lists of the most popular tools in relevant categories (niche industries can have their own tools and Web sites). While the categories and tools can change over time, the tools here are the most popular, broad-based tools available and most likely used in an organizational environment.

Blog Platforms and Communities

Blog platforms (software) and their respective communities are designed for the creation and management of blogs. These tools support the authoring and publishing of content, comments, as well as site management tools.

> Blogger (free)
>> www.blogger.com
>
> TypePad (paid)
>> www.typepad.com
>
> SharePoint (paid)
>> sharepoint.microsoft.com
>
> SocialText (paid)
>> www.socialtext.com
>
> SquareSpace (paid)
>> www.squarespace.com
>
> Windows Live Spaces (free)
>> home.spaces.live.com
>
> Wordpress (hosted version; free)
>> www.wordpress.com
>
> Wordpress (free downloadable software; requires hosting)
>> www.wordpress.org (free blog community software)
>
> Wordpress Multi User (requires hosting)
>> mu.wordpress.org

Microblogging and Status Updates

The major differentiators between microblogging (and status updates) from traditional blogging are the length of the content and the real-time nature of the content. Most long-form blog content is generally greater than 200 words; microblogs and status updates generally range from 140 characters to a couple of sentences, or could simply be an image or short video segment.

Additionally, this shorter form of content is more about events that are occurring "right now" and might include personal updates, news events as they occur, or information being presented during a conference.

Facebook (status updates)
www.Facebook.com
LinkedIn (status updates)
www.LinkedIn.com
MySpace (status updates)
www.myspace.com
Ning (custom network creation; paid subscription))
www.ning.com
Plurk (microblogging)
www.plurk.com (microblogging)
Posterous
www.posterous.com
SocialText (microblogging)
www.socialtext.com
Twitter.com (microblogging)
www.twitter.com
Yammer (enterprise microblogging)
www.yammer.com

Forums and Discussion Groups

What started as early electronic bulletin board systems, discussion groups, and forums have become a popular method of connecting and conversing about a seemingly endless number of topics.

Facebook Groups
www.Facebook.com
Google Groups
groups.google.com
LinkedIn Groups
www.LinkedIn.com

SocialText

www.socialtext.com

Yahoo Groups

groups.yahoo.com

There are countless other sites available, including internal discussion forums for employees and stakeholders. A content-specific search would need to be done to determine the most appropriate for a particular topic or organization.

Social Media Networks

These sites represent the largest and most influential social networking platforms as of mid-2010. Though the overall global list is extensive, these are the platforms that have developed the largest global social networking footprint. Each of these enables like-minded people to connect, create and share content, and join in conversations that are relevant to their interests.

Bebo (owned by AOL)

www.bebo.com

Facebook

www.Facebook.com

LinkedIn

www.LinkedIn.com

MyLife (formerly reunion.com)

www.mylife.com

My Space (owned by News Corp)

www.myspace.com

Reviews and Ratings Services

Review and rating sites (whether they be stand-alone or tied to an e-commerce platform) are based on user-generated content in the form of feedback, opinions, and ratings regarding businesses, products, and services.

These sites significantly impact consumer behavior. According to a 2007 Comscore/Kelsey Research study, "consumers were willing to pay at least 20 percent more for services receiving an 'Excellent,' or 5-star, rating than for the same service receiving a 'Good,' or 4-star, rating." Additionally, "nearly one out of every four Internet users (24 percent) reported using online reviews before paying for a service delivered offline."

Amazon
    www.amazon.com
Epinions
    www.epinions.com
TripAdvisor
    www.tripadvisor.com
Yelp
    www.yelp.com

Photo Sharing

Photo sharing sites allow individuals to upload and host their images, connect with each other, and provide feedback and comments on photographs. Some services allow for content to be repurposed under a creative commons license, while others offer a payment for the licensing of an image.

Flickr (owned by Yahoo!) (free and pro accounts)
    www.flickr.com
SmugMug (free and pro accounts)
    www.smugmug.com
PhotoBucket (owned by News Corp; free)
    www.photobucket.com
Picasa (owned by Google; free photo editor)
    www.picasa.com

Video Sharing

Much like photo sharing sites, video sharing sites allow individuals to upload and host videos and, in most cases, embed them into other online applications such as Web sites, blogs, social networking platforms, and so on.

Blip.tv

www.blip.tv (also distributes content to other video sharing networks)

Flickr (owned by Yahoo!; free and pro accounts)

www.flickr.com

Revver

www.revver.com

YouTube (owned by Google)

www.YouTube.com

Viddler

www.viddler.com

Vimeo

www.vimeo.com

Podcasting

Podcasts are audio and/or video files that can be downloaded for playback via computer or a digital music device such as an mp3 player, iPod, Zune, and so on. Podcasts are generally similar to nonbroadcast (or rebroadcasts) radio programming. Most are episodic in nature and tend to focus on a particular topic. While it is up to the publisher to create the content, the following are the most popular sources to distribute that content.

iTunes (owned by Apple)

www.apple.com/itunes

PodCastAlley

www.podcastalley.com

Customer Service

Though customer service issues are generally dealt with on the organization's site (using either third-party or proprietary applications), there are hosted solutions that have an element of social media integration. This integration generally allows customers to see, help answer, and provide feedback on product and/or customer service issues. This not only can add an additional layer of transparency to an organization's customer service efforts, but can also serve as a valuable feedback system and a way to collect ideas on product improvements and innovations.

> Get Statisfaction (paid subscription)
>> www.getsatisfaction.com
> Crowd Sound (paid subscription)
>> www.crowdsound.com
> Salesforce (paid subscription)
>> www.salesforce.com

Document and Content Sharing

These sites allow individuals to upload documents, presentations, white papers, and the like for private, group, or public sharing. In some instances, these sites can also facilitate paid downloads or serve as lead generation mechanisms. Over the past few years, these sites have gained in popularity as a way to freely distribute thought leadership, white papers, product information, case studies, and slide decks from conference sessions or workshops.

> DocStoc
>> www.docstoc.com
> Google Docs
>> docs.google.com

Scribd

www.scribd.com

SlideShare

www.slideshare.net

Zoho

www.zoho.com

Events and Event Management

These sites help meeting organizers set up, manage, and promote events. Some of these sites also have group elements that allows them to join real-word or virtual clubs and participate in offline events. Depending on the level of promotion desired, meeting organizers can publicly list events or syndicate content through various social networks.

EventBrite

www.eventbrite.com

Facebook Events

www.Facebook.com

MeetUp

www.meetup.com

Upcoming

www.upcoming.com

Knowledge Management (wikis) and Project Management

Wikis allow for the easy cocreation of content by one or multiple publishers using a simple text editor, thereby empowering the creation and editing of content by publishers that do not have extensive HTML or programming experience. Wikis are often used to power consumer-generated content that is refined over time by individual publishers, such as the open-source encycopedia Wikipedia, but are also commonly used for corporate intranets/extranets, virtual work teams, and in knowledge management systems.

Social project management systems allow individuals or groups to participate and collaborate on particular projects.

BaseCamp
    www.37signals.com
PBWorks
    www.pbwiki.com
SocialText
    www.socialtext.com
Wikia
    www.wikia.com
Wikipedia
    www.wikipedia.org

Social Bookmarking

Social bookmarking allows users to create, store, and share bookmarks for online Web pages. Similar to the bookmarking feature found on Internet browsers, these sites are hosted by a third party and incorporate the social features of sharing, rating, and using a tag-based folksonomy to organize and classify content.

Delicious (formerly del.icio.us)
    www.delicious.com
Stumble Upon
    www.stumbleupon.com
InstaPaper
    www.instapaper.com

Location-Based Services

Social media location-based services (LBS) are generally applications on mobile devices that combine the social aspects of connecting and sharing information with the geographical location of the person. Though there are a number of non-social applications, social LBS applications involve a check-in from an individual to a particular location (home, work, retailer, etc.).

Though relatively new to the social media landscape, the ability to discover businesses and friends in close proximity, read reviews, receive cash incentives, coupons, or play games has been very appealing to early adopters. As of mid-2010, LBS applications are being developed that integrate elements of social media with loyalty and incentive programs, mobile commerce, UPC scanning, and comparison-shopping engines.

Facebook Places

www.Facebook.com

Foursquare

www.foursquare.com

Gowalla

gowalla.com

Loopt

www.loopt.com

WeReward

www.wereward.com

Yelp

www.yelp.com

Common and Popular Social Media Monitoring Tools

We understand that the following is a fairly long list of monitoring tools, but it is not exhaustive. Because the foundation of social media is based on listening, learning, and monitoring, the idea here is that you cannot listen enough to what is being said about and by the brand, stakeholders, industry, and competition. These can also be invaluable to help audit the social media content created by stakeholders (primarily current or former staff and vendors) to ensure that information is not being inappropriately disclosed.

These tools have a wide array of features, some better suited for various organizations or business units than others. For those that are based on a paid subscription, most, if not all, offer a free evaluation to determine which is the most appropriate for the need. Our recommendation is to have someone in your organization review (or at least scan) each of them, identifying the ones with the best fit. It is also worthwhile to test a few to determine the accurate, adequacy, and timeliness for your needs.

Addictomatic
    addictomatic.com
AIM
    newmediastrategies.net

Alterian
>socialmedia.alterian.com

Analytic.ly
>analytics.peoplebrowsr.com

Asomo
>www.asomo.net

Attentio
>attentio.com

Awareness Networks
>www.awarenessnetworks.com/software/measure

Backtype
>www.backtype.com

Beevolve
>www.beevolve.com

Blog Grader
>blog.grader.com

Blogpulse
>www.blogpulse.com

Boardreader
>boardreader.com

BrandMetric
>www.brandmetric.com

Brands Eye
>www.brandseye.com

Brandtology
>www.brandtology.com

Brandwatch
>www.brandwatch.com/solutions

Buzz Numbers HQ
>www.buzznumbershq.com

Buzzcapture
>www.buzzcapture.com

BuzzGain
>www.BuzzGain.com/index.html

Buzzient Enterprise
    www.buzzient.com
BuzzLogic Insight
    www.buzzlogic.com
BuzzPerception
    www.customscoop.com/products/buzzperception.php
BuzzStream
    www.buzzstream.com
Cision Social Media
    us.cision.com
ClipIQ
    www.customscoop.com
Cognito Monitor
    www.expertsystem.net
Collecta
    Collecta.com
Collective Intellect
    www.collectiveintellect.com/products/self_service
Context Voice
    contextvoice.com/applications
Conversation
    www.ecairn.com
Conversation Miner
    www.converseon.com/us/services/services1.html
CoTweet
    www.cotweet.com
Crimson Hexagon
    www.crimsonhexagon.com/product
Custom Scoop
    www.customscoop.com
Cyber Alert
    www.cyberalert.com
Cyveillance
    www.cyveillance.com

Dialogix
> www.dialogix.com/.au

Digimind Meta-Search
> www.digimind.com/products

Direct Message Lab
> www.directmessagelab.com

dnaMonitor
> www.dna13.com

Dow Jones Insight
> www.dowjones.com/product-djinsight.asp

Evolve 24
> evolve24.com/products-services/the-mirror

eWatch
> ewatch.prnewswire.com

Facebook Grader
> facebook.grader.com

Feedburner
> feedburner.google.com

Filtrbox
> www.filtrbox.com

Followthing
> followthing.com

Gnip
> gnip.com

Google Blogsearch
> blogsearch.google.com

Graph Edge
> www.graphedge.com

HowSociable
> howsociable.com

Hubspot
> www.hubspot.com/marketing-tools

Icerocket
> www.icerocket.com

iCrossing
    www.icrossing.com/marketing-platform
Impactwatch
    impactwatch.com
Just Signal
    justsignal.com
Klout
    klout.com
Linkfluence
    linkfluence.net
Livedash
    www.livedash.com
Looxii
    www.looxii.com
Loudpixel
    loudpixel.com
Maestro
    www.cymfony.com/Solutions/Cymfony-Maestro
Managing News
    managingnews.com
Market Sentinel
    www.marketsentinel.com
Market Voice
    www.attensity.com
Marketo
    www.marketo.com
Media Genius
    www.mediageniusapp.com
MediaMiser Enterprise
    www.mediamiser.com/products/enterprise.html
Mediasphere360
    www.mediabadger.com
Meltwater
    www.meltwater.com/products/meltwater-buzz

Mentionmap
    apps.asterisq.com/mentionmap/#
Meteor
    www.meteorsolutions.com
Metrica
    www.metrica.net/Whatwedo/Content2l.htm
Monitter
    www.monitter.com
Motive Quest
    www.motivequest.com/main.taf?p=1,2
My BuzzMetrics
    en-us.nielsen.com/tab/product_families/nielsen_
    buzzmetrics
My Reputation Manager
    reputationhq.com/
Newsdesk
    moreover.com/public/products/newsdesk.html
Omniture
    www.omniture.com
Onalytica
    onalytica.com
OneRiot
    www.oneriot.com
Open Mic
    www.overtone.com/product/open-mic
Optify
    www.optify.net
Positive Press
    www.iterasi.net
Post Rank
    www.postrank.com
Radian6
    www.radian6.com

Raven
   raven-seo-tools.com
Reputation Control
   www.reputation-control.de
Reputation Defender
   www.reputationdefender.com
RepuTrace
   www.repumetrix.com
Resonate
   www.listenlogic.com/solutions/resonate.php
Revinate
   www.revinate.com
RightNow
   www.rightnow.com/cx-suite-social-experience.php
SAS
   www.sas.com/software/customer-intelligence/social-
   media-analytics
Scanbuzz
   www.medimix.net/content/scanbuzz-services
ScoutLabs
   www.scoutlabs.com
Sentiment Metrics
   www.sentimentmetrics.com
Silverbakk Briefing Room
   www.silverbakk.com
SM2
   www.alterian-social-media.com
Snapstream
   www.snapstream.com/enterprise
Social Media Dashboard
   www.ovrdrv.com
Social Mention
   socialmention.com

Social Radar
    www.infegy.com/socialradar.php
Social Too
    socialtoo.com
SocialMetrix
    www.SocialMetrix.com
Socialscape
    www.socialscape.biz
SocialSeek
    www.sensidea.com/socialseek
SocialSense
    www.net/workedinsights.com/products
Socialtalk
    www.socialtalk.com
SpredFast
    spredfast.com
StartPR
    startpr.com
StatsMix
    statsmix.com
Steprep
    steprep.myfrontsteps.com
Symscio
    www.symscio.com/PR_Measurement/Dashboards
Synthesio
    www.synthesio.com/corporate/gb_index.php
Sysomos MAP & Heartbeat
    www.sysomos.com/products/overview/sysomos-map
Systemone Radar
    www.systemone.net/en/products/radar
Tealium SM
    www.tealium.com/products/social-media/index.html
The Search Monitor
    www.thesearchmonitor.com

ThoughtBuzz
    www.thoughtbuzz.net

TraceBuzz
    www.tracebuzz.com

Trackur
    www.trackur.com

Trendistic
    trendistic.com

Trendrr
    www.trendrr.com

Tribe Monitor
    https:/www.tribemonitor.com

TruReach
    www.visiblemeasures.com

TweetBeep
    www.tweetbeep.com

TweetFeel
    www.tweetfeel.com

Twitalyzer
    www.twitalyzer.com

Twitter Grader
    twitter.grader.com

Twitter Search
    search.twitter.com

Umbria
    www.jdpowerwebintelligence.com

Viralheat
    www.viralheat.com

Visible
    www.visibletechnologies.com/products.html

Vitrue
    vitrue.com/smi

Vocus PR
    www.vocus.com/content/social-media.asp

Web Clipping
www.webclipping.com
Webdig
www.woollabs.com/Webdig.html
WebTrends
www.webtrends.com/Products/SocialMeasurement
White Noise
www.herdthenoise.com
Whitevector
www.whitevector.com
Who's Talkin
www.whostalkin.com
Woopra
www.woopra.com
Workstreamer
www.workstreamer.com/social

APPENDIX D

Links to Publicly Available Social Media Policies

The following list is intended to provide the reader a quick reference to some of the social media policies that are available to the public. These represent policies that show some of the attributes we have been discussing. No one of these will be perfect for your situation, but each will provide insight and guidance on how your company may want to approach development of a social media policy

American Institute of Architects

www.aia.org/about/AIAB083034

American Red Cross: Local guidelines

docs.google.com/View?docid=df4n5v7k_216g5jdd
7c8&hgd=1

Best Buy

www.bby.com/2010/01/20/best-buy-social-media-guidelines/

Cisco

blogs.cisco.com/news/comments/ciscos_internet_postings_
policy

City of Seattle

www.seattle.gov/pan/SocialMediaPolicy.htm

Cleveland Clinic

  my.clevelandclinic.org/social_media_policy.aspx

Coca-Cola

  www.viralblog.com/wp-content/uploads/2010/01/TCCC-
  Online-Social-Media-Principles-12–2009.pdf

Daimler AG

  www.daimler.com/Projects/c2c/channel/documents/
  1895107_Social_Media_Guidelines_eng_Final.pdf

Dell

  www.dell.com/content/topics/global.aspx/policy/en/
  policy?c=us&l=en&s=corp&~section=019

DePaul University

  brandresources.depaul.edu/vendor_guidelines/g_socialme-
  dia.aspx

Easter Seals

  www.easterseals.com/site/PageServer?pagename=ntlc8_
  community_guidelines

Flickr

  www.flickr.com/guidelines.gne

Ford Motor Company

  www.scribd.com/doc/36127480/Ford-Social-Media-Guidelines

Gartner

  blogs.gartner.com/?page_id=69

General Services Administration

  www.gsa.gov/graphics/staffoffices/socialmediapolicy.pdf

Get Satisfaction

  getsatisfaction.com/ccpact

General Motors

  fastlane.gmblogs.com/about.html

Harvard Law School

    blogs.law.harvard.edu/terms-of-use

Hill & Knowlton

    www.hillandknowlton.com/principles

HP

    www.hp.com/hpinfo/blogs/codeofconduct.html

IBM

    www.ibm.com/blogs/zz/en/guidelines.html

Intel

    www.intel.com/sites/sitewide/en_US/social-media.htm

Kaiser Permanente

    xnet.kp.org/newscenter/media/downloads/
    socialmediapolicy_091609.pdf

Kodak

    www.kodak.com/US/images/en/corp/aboutKodak/online-
    Today/Kodak_SocialMediaTips_Aug14.pdf

Mayo Clinic

    sharing.mayoclinic.org/guidelines/for-mayo-clinic-employees

Microsoft

    socialmediagovernance.com/MSFT_Social_Media_Policy.pdf

National Public Radio (NPR)

    www.npr.org/about/ethics/social_media_guidelines.html

Nordstrom

    shop.nordstrom.com/c/social-networking-guidelines

Ogilvy

    blog.ogilvypr.com/2010/02/empowering-communicators-
    via-a-social-media-policy

Oracle/Sun

    www.sun.com/communities/guidelines.jsp

Porter Novelli

www.scribd.com/doc/3964369/Porter-Novelli-Blogging-and-Social-Media-Policy-v02

Razorfish

www.razorfish.com/img/content/RazorfishSIMguideWeb July2009.pdf

Right Now Technologies

www.rightnow.com

SAP

www.scribd.com/doc/17249115/SAP-Social-Media-Participation-Guidelines-2009

Salesforce.com

www.slideshare.net/Salesforce/salesforce-social-media -policy-6–10

Sentara

www.sentara.com/Policies/Pages/SocialMediaPolicy.aspx

Thompson Reuters

handbook.reuters.com/index.php/Reporting_from_the _internet#Social_media_guidelines

U.S. Air Force

www.af.mil/shared/media/document/AFD-090406–036.pdf

U.S. Coast Guard

www.af.mil/shared/media/document/AFD-090406–036.pdf

U.S. Department of Defense

socialmedia.defense.gov/about

University of Michigan

voices.umich.edu/docs/Social-Media-Guidelines.pdf

University of Oregon

www.communications.uoregon.edu/socialmedia

Vanderbilt University

> www.vanderbilt.edu/publicaffairs/webcomm/social-media
> -handbook

Walmart

> walmartstores.com/9179.aspx

Webtrends

> blog.webtrends.com/about/social-media-guidelines

Wells Fargo

> blog.wellsfargo.com/community-guidelines.html

Links and Information Regarding Regulation, Guidelines, and Legal Issues Involving Social Media

There are certain guidelines that have been specifically developed to address social media and have been listed below. However, with social media being a communications channel, there are many existing laws, regulations, and guidelines that will come into play throughout the world. Because we are not attorneys and cannot advise in all the applicable laws and their specific implications with social media, our recommendation is to work closely with the legal, risk, and compliance teams to ensure that any general communications risks have also been addressed as they apply to social media.

Areas where legal or regulatory implications could affect social media include (this is a general overview and not comprehensive to locality, industry, etc.):

- Copyright and trademark infringement.
- Defamation, tort, and criminal activity.
- Employment discrimination practices (for existing and prospective employees).
- SEC regulations and financial disclosure requirements.
- Privacy and confidentiality concerns (especially HIPAA).

- Information storage and data access.
- Marketing and advertising to minors.

Specific Guidelines that Apply to Social Media

- Federal Trade Commission: Covering endorsements, testimonials, and disclosure: www.ftc.gov/opa/2009/10/endortest .shtm
- FINRA: Guidance on blogs and social networking Web sites: www.finra.org/Industry/Regulation/Notices/2010/P120760

White Papers and Thought Leadership

- Social Media Risks and Rewards, Reed Smith: www.reed-smith.com/publications.cfm?cit_id=27280&widCall1=custo mWidgets.content_view_1&usecache=false
- When Marketing through Social Media, Legal Risks Can Go Viral, Venable: www.venable.com/files/Publication/ b4f467b9–0666–4b36-b021–351540962d65/Presentation/ PublicationAttachment/019f4e5f-d6f8–4eeb-af43– 40a4323b9ff1/Social_Media_white_paper.pdf
- Legal Issues in Social Networking, Miller Canfield Paddock and Stone PLC: www.millercanfield.com/media/article/ 200120_LEGAL%20ISSUES%20IN%20SOCIAL%20NETWOR KING.pdf

About the Authors

Peter R. Scott, APR, is a senior-level social media and public relations strategist, working with some of the world's largest and most respected brands and agencies. For more than 15 years, Peter has led numerous communications, marketing, and interactive media, including serving as the director of Marketing and Web Operations for The Institute of Internal Auditors.

J. Mike Jacka, CIA, CPCU, CLU, CPA, has worked in internal auditing since 1983. He has been involved in all aspects of the profession, including development of fraud protocols and procedures, development of a training curriculum and materials for a 200-person audit shop, design of continuous audit techniques used to streamline field audit processes, and management of a 30-person department.

Mike has been involved with The Institute of Internal Auditors (IIA) for more than 10 years. For much of that time, he has been a member of the International Editorial Policy Committee and a volunteer instructor for IIA seminars. He is a popular speaker on such topics as process mapping, tools for operational auditing, auditors and creativity, and, of course, social media. He is coauthor of the book *Business Process Mapping: Improving Customer Satisfaction* and is currently responsible for "The Lighter Side" articles published in *The Internal Auditor,* including such pieces as "High Noon in Tombstone, Inc.," "Auditors Anonymous," and "Alice in Auditland." His blog, "From the Mind of Mike Jacka," can also be found at the *Internal Auditor* Web site, www.theiia .org/blogs/jacka/.

Mike can be reached by e-mail at figre@cox.net and if you're really bored, you can follow his obscure ramblings on Twitter @Figre. (The less said about that, the better.)

Index